TALK DIRTY
YIDDISH

BEYOND DREK: THE CURSES, SLANG, AND STREET LINGO
YOU NEED TO KNOW WHEN YOU SPEAK YIDDISH

TALK DIRTY
YIDDISH

ILENE SCHNEIDER

adamsmedia
Avon, Massachusetts

Published by
Adams Media, an F+W Publications Company
57 Littlefield Street, Avon, MA 02322
www.adamsmedia.com

ISBN 13: 978-1-59869-856-5
ISBN 10: 1-59869-856-7

Printed in Canada.

J I H G F E D C B A

Library of Congress Cataloging-in-Publication Data
is available from the publisher.

This publication is designed to provide accurate and authoritative information with regard to the subject matter covered. It is sold with the unders-
tanding that the publisher is not engaged in rendering legal, accounting, or
other professional advice. If legal advice or other expert assistance is required, the services of a competent professional person should be sought.
   —From a *Declaration of Principles* jointly adopted by a Committee of the
American Bar Association and a Committee of Publishers and Associations

Many of the designations used by manufacturers and sellers to distinguish
their product are claimed as trademarks. Where those designations appear
in this book and Adams Media was aware of a trademark claim, the designations have been printed with initial capital letters.

Interior illustrations ©iStockphoto.com/Matt Knannlein.

This book is available at quantity discounts for bulk purchases.
For information, please call 1-800-289-0963.

This book is dedicated to all those who spoke the rich, colorful, dynamic language known as Yiddish, and to those who are committed to keeping the language just as alive and vibrant today.

Contents

Acknowledgments

My appreciation goes to Paula Munier, acquisitions editor of Adams Media, who had faith that I could write this book, to her assistant, Sara Stock, who shepherded me through the process, and to Katrina Schroeder, who shaped the manuscript into its final form.

My thanks to those who did not want to be acknowledged by name, but gave me words and phrases and advice.

Thanks to my mother, whose own mother was more comfortable speaking in Yiddish than English, for her memories of her childhood. And to my father who, despite having grown up with parents who did not speak Yiddish and a grandmother who did not want to speak it, still picked up a lot of phrases.

And profound, deep gratitude to my husband, Rabbi Gary M. Gans, who proofread the manuscript, and gave me ideas and suggestions, and caught all my typos. I could not have produced this book without him.

Preface

This book will not teach you how to speak Yiddish. Instead, it will teach you various idiomatic phrases and colloquial vocabulary words that can be sprinkled in your conversation to enrich and enliven it, to give it some texture and interest.

In addition, the words are not just listed by subject matter and then translated. There are mini-essays scattered among the definitions that add a sociological and historical context to the vocabulary. The information will help non-Jews understand the milieu in which Yiddish developed and flourished, and contains some little known facts and trivia to interest knowledgeable readers.

It has been my intention to present a book that is both informative and entertaining, without being either too academic or too superficial. I hope I have succeeded.

Talking Dirty ... in Yiddish?

How to talk dirty—in Yiddish? I always thought it could not be done, that there are curses but not curse words in Yiddish. But Yiddish does have vulgarisms, coarse language, colorful insults, and offensive words. It even has the equivalent of four-letter Anglo-Saxon "expletive deleteds." This book will teach you how to use them all—but will not guarantee that you will still have any friends afterwards.

Shortly after being asked to write this book, I was at a conference attended by several Yiddish speakers, and mentioned the project to some I met. Their universal reaction was: "How to talk dirty in Yiddish? Can't be done." My informants were all women "of a certain age," and professional Yiddishists and linguists. When I mentioned the topic of the book to casual Yiddish speakers, I found out it can be done, but not in public.

As one woman at the conference explained to me, "Who did I learn Yiddish from? My mother. She'd never use such words. So I don't know any. Well, there is '*Lig in dred*,' but that's all." The phrase means literally, "Lay in the ground," or "Drop dead." Not exactly dirty, but as dirty as she had ever heard.

Another woman at the conference agreed: "My mother had sex once. That's how I got born. When she went to the gynecologist, she described her symptoms as being *dorten*, 'down there.'" She did provide me with two examples, however: "*Gai kaken in dem yam*," literally "Go shit in the ocean," or "Get lost;" and "*Gai tren zich,*" or "Go fuck yourself." I suspect that she was embarrassed that she knew these phrases, and was probably worried her mother would rise up from the grave to wash her mouth out with soap.

Someone else told me the only dirty word she could think of (and it was in English) was "cancer." The word was always referred to obliquely, in hushed tones. "Did you hear? He has you-know-what."

But what they did not consider was that words like *shiksa* (a non-Jewish woman) or *shaigits* (a non-Jewish man) could be perceived as offensive. To many Yiddish speakers, these words are merely descriptive, but there is an implication of disdain that make them as taboo as *drek* (shit).

The word *drek* is illustrative of the transformation that occurred when many Yiddish words and phrases made their way into English. These words became innocuous replacements for the equivalent Anglo-Saxon words. Lenny Bruce is credited with having brought these words into the mainstream of English usage when he realized that the censors, who would have him kicked off the stage for saying "prick," had no idea that *shmuck* meant the same thing.

Of the approximately eight hundred words and phrases in this book, about sixty are considered "impolite" and only fifteen of those are considered truly obscene. (George Carlin was able to identify a measly seven in English.) But I would not recommend using them or the other forty-five rude words in polite society . . . unless you want your mother to wash your mouth out with soap.

CHAPTER ONE

A Brokh Tsu Dayn Lebn!

Curses and Curse Words

It may seem as though it should be easy to "talk dirty" in a language with over sixty vulgarisms, but ask many Yiddish speakers and they will say they do not know any curse words. (There is a gender division here: the women don't know any—or won't admit they do—while the men say they know quite a few.) No one, however, will deny that Yiddish is replete with wonderful curses.

A curse is not the same as a curse word. I was looking for a book on Yiddish curses that I knew we owned, and could not find it on our bookshelves. I finally found it in my then thirteen-year-old son's room, under his bed. He had thought he would be able to learn from its pages how to say the "S-word" without being reprimanded. Much to his disappointment, the book contains lists of curses, not curse words.

A curse word is an expletive; it is the expression you use when you hit your thumb with a hammer and yell, "Fuck!" A curse is a hex. It is when you wish someone ill, as in the oft quoted "May you grow like an onion, with your head in the ground."

In Yiddish, cursing, in the sense of casting a spell, is a time-honored tradition. Entire books have been devoted to lists of curses, covering all types of situations. If you have daughters, "They should be like the flowers of the field—wither and fade away." If you have sons, "They should be so smart that they learn the Mourner's Prayer before their *Bar Mitzvah* portions" (i.e., you should die before they turn thirteen). If your health is good, "You should outlive everyone but your mother-in-law." (Mother-in-law jokes, it seems, are universal.) If you are wealthy, "All your competitors' stores should burn down except yours, and yours should burn down the day the insurance lapses."

Some curses can be quite vulgar. For example, you would not hear "You should crap glass and piss vinegar" in polite company. But most Yiddish curses are in the category of humorous, although mean-spirited, wishes. Especially clever are the ones that start out sounding like a blessing: "Your chickens should lay many eggs each day…in your neighbor's yard"; "You should never develop stomach trouble…from too rich a diet"; "You should have many descendants…and have to support them all"; "God should answer all your prayers…and then mistake your worst enemy for you."

Yiddish curses are often translated into English translations using the phrase "may you," but that is much more polite than the literal Yiddish. In Yiddish, curses generally begin with or include the word *zol*, which means should. The formulation is seen as *zol er* (he should), *zol zi* (she should), *zol es* (it should), *zoln* (they should), or, if you are confronting your antagonist in person, *zolst* (you should), as in the universal parental lament, "You should only have children like you so you should know what it is like."

A curse in English like "Go to Hell" (which has a Yiddish equivalent: *Gai in drerd arein!*) pales beside a curse in Yiddish like "Your enemies should get cramps in their legs from dancing on your grave." Who needs curse words when you have such inventive curses instead?

Imprecations

Here is a sampling of creative Yiddish curses. There are more scattered throughout other chapters of the book.

Brokh
Curse

A brokh!
Oh hell! Damn it!

A brokh iz mir!
I am cursed!

A brokh tsu dayn lebn!
A curse on your life!

A brokh tsu dayn lebn, nish fahr dir degakht!
A curse on your life, may it never happen to you!

A brokh tsu dir!
A curse on you!

A feier zol im trefn!
He should burn up!

A kholaire af dir!
A cholera on you!

A meshugener zol men oyshraybn, un im araynshraybn.
They should free a madman, and lock him up instead.

A mise meshune af dir!
An unnatural death on you!

A shvarts yor af dir!
A difficult year on you!

Azoy fil ritzinoyl zol er oystrinkn.
He should drink too much castor oil.

3

Brenen zol er!
He should burn (in hell)!

Brenen zolst afn fayer!
You should burn in fire!

Es iz nit geshtoygen un nit gefloygen!
It never rose and it never flew! (The English version would be:
They ran it up the flag pole and no one saluted. It was a bullshit
idea.)

Fahrshporn zol er oyf shtain?
Why should he bother to get up alive?

Finstere laid zol nor di mama oyf im zen.
Black sorrow is all that his mother should see of him.

Gai avek!
Go away!

Gai in drerd arein!
Go to hell!

Gai plats!
Go blow up!

Gai shoyn, gai!
Go away already!

Gai strashe di vantsn!
Go threaten the bedbugs. (In other words, you don't scare me!)

Heng dikh oyf a tsikershtrikl vestu hobn a zisn toyt.
Hang yourself with a sugar rope and you'll have a sweet death.
(Similar to "hoisted on his own petard.")

Ikh fayf af dir!
I whistle on you! (In colloquial English, I wash my hands of you.)

Ikh hob es in drerd!
To hell with it!

Hindert hayzer zol er hobn, in yeder hoyz a hindert tsimern, in yeder tsimer tsvonsik betn un kadukhes zol im varfn fin ain bet in der tsvaiter.
A hundred houses he should have, in every house a hundred rooms and in every room twenty beds, and a delirious fever should drive him from bed to bed.

Ikh hob im in bod!
To hell with him!

Ikh hob dikh in bod!
I'll have you in the bath! (In other words, watch your back. I'll get you when you least expect it.)

Ikh hob dir!
I have you! (I know what you're up to. Drop dead!)

Ikh hob es in drerd!
To hell with it!

In di zumerdike teg zol er zitsn shive, un in di vinterdike nekht zikh raysn af di tsain.
On summer days he should mourn, and on wintry nights, he should torture himself.

Khasene hobn zol er mit di malekh hamoves tokhter.
He should marry the daughter of the Angel of Death.

Lakhn zol er mit yashtherkes.
He should laugh with lizards. (Lizards aren't known for laughing, so he should never laugh or be happy again.)

Lig in drerd!
Lay in the ground! Bury yourself! Get lost! Drop dead!

Loz mikh tsu ru!
Leave me in peace; leave me alone!

Makeh.
Plague, disease.

A makeh af dir!
A plague on you!

A makeh in yenems oren iz nit shver tzu trogen.
Another's disease isn't hard to endure.

A mol iz der refueh erger fun der makeh.
Sometimes the cure is worse than the disease.

Er zol hobn paroys makehs bashotn mit oybes krets.
He should have Pharaoh's plagues sprinkled with Job's scabies.

Fransn zol esn zayn layb.
Venereal disease should consume his body.

Got zol oyf im onshikn fin di tsen makes di beste.
God should visit upon him the best of the Ten Plagues.

Migulgl zol er vern in a henglayhter, by tog zol er hengen, un bay nakht zol er brenen.
He should be transformed into a chandelier, by day he should hang, and by night he should burn.

Nem zikh a vane!
Take a bath! (In English we'd say, Go jump in the lake!)

Oyf doktoyrim zol er dos avekgebn.
He should give it (his money) all away to doctors.

Oyskrenkn zol er dus mame's milakh.
He should get so sick as to cough up his mother's milk.

Shtainer zol zi hobn, nit kain kinder.
Stones she should have, and not children.

Trinkn zoln im piavkes.
Leeches should drink him dry.

Vi tsu derleb ikh im shoyn tsu bagrobn.
I should outlive him long enough to bury him.

Zai nit kain Vayzoso!
Don't be Vayzoso (one of Haman's sons)! (Don't be a fool! Don't be a *shmuck!*)

Zol er krenken un gedenken.
He should suffer and remember.

Zol er lebn—oder nit lang.
He should live—but not long.

Zol er vern dershtikt.
He should be strangled.

Zol er vern gesharget.
He should be murdered.

Zol er brenem in gehenem.
He should burn in Hell.

Zol es im onkumn vos ikh vintsh im, khotsh a helft, khotsh halb, khotsh a tsent khailik.
What I wish on him should come true, most, even half, even just ten percent.

Zolst habn a ziser toyt—a vagon mit tsuker zol dir iberforn.
You should have a sweet death—a wagon full of sugar should run you over.

Zolst habn a zun vos men ruft nokh dir—un in gikhn.
You should have a son named for you—and soon. (Ashkenazi Jews name their children after someone who is deceased.)

CHAPTER TWO

A Shprikhvort Iz a Vorvort.
A Proverb Is a True Word

Wherever spoken language existed, so did proverbs, aphorisms, maxims, and words of wisdom. Not only are they are known in every language and society throughout the world, but they are considered a vibrant part of those cultures' folklore. Proverbs were already an ancient oral tradition when King Solomon began collecting them in the second half of the tenth century B.C.E. The earliest ones have been traced to twenty-sixth century B.C.E Egypt, and Aristotle considered them the remnants of an older philosophy.

Yiddish has thousands of proverbs and sayings. Pithy, humorous, wise, with a central kernel of truth, many Yiddish proverbs are translated from Polish, Russian, or other languages familiar to Jews living in those countries. Many sayings and proverbs are scattered throughout this book. Below is just a small sampling of some others. Some are familiar words of wisdom to English speakers; others should be. They all fit the definition of a proverb: a concise phrase that encapsulates a universal truth.

A falsheh matba'ieh fahrliert men nit.
A bad penny always turns up.

A guten vet der shaink vit kalyeh makh, un a shlekhtne vet der bes-hamedresh nit fairkhtn.
A good person won't be made bad by a tavern, and a bad one won't be reformed by the synagogue.

A gutter feint iz oft besser fun a bruder.
A good friend is often better than a brother.

A katz meg oikh kuken oifen kaisser.
A cat can look at a king.

A ligner dark hoben a guten zekhron.
A liar needs a good memory.

A ligner hert zikh zeine ligen azoi lang ein biz er glaibt zikh alain.
A liar tells his story so often even he believes it.

Proverbs sometimes contradict each other. In English we have both, "Distance makes the heart grow fonder," and "Out of sight, out of mind." In Yiddish, there's A freint bekamt men umzist; a soineh muz men zikh koifn. (A friend you get for nothing; an enemy has to be bought.), and A freint darf men zikh koifn; sonem krigt men umzist. (A friend you have to buy; enemies you get for nothing.)

A nar bleibt a nar.
A fool remains a fool.

A nar fahrlirt un a kluger gefint.
A fool loses and a clever man finds.

A nar gait in bod arein un fahrgest zikh dos ponim optzuvashn.

A fool goes to the baths and forgets to wash his face.

A nar gait tzvai mol dort, vu a kluger gait nit kain aintzik mol.

A fool goes twice, while a clever man doesn't go even once.

A nar git, a kluger nemt.

A fool gives, a wise man takes.

A nar ken a mol zogen a gleikh vort.

Even a fool can sometimes say something clever.

A shlekhte sholem iz besser vi a gutter krig.

A bad peace is better than a good war.

Aider me zogt arois s'vort, iz men a har; dernokh iz men a nar.

Before you say a word you're a master; afterwards, you're a fool.

Az dos hartz iz ful, gai'en di oygen iber.

When the heart is full, the eyes overflow.

Az meshiakh vet kumen, vellen alleh krankeh oisgehailt verren; nor a nar vet bleiben a nar.

When the Messiah comes, all the sick will be healed; only a fool will stay a fool.

Az ikh vel zein vi yener, ver vet zein vi ikh?

If I would be like someone else, who would be like me?

Az me muz, ken men.

When one must, one can. (In other words, necessity is the mother of invention.)

Az men ken nit iberharn dos shlekhteh, ken men dos guteh nit derleben.

If you can't endure the bad, you won't live to witness the good.

Az se brent, iz a fei'er:
Where there's smoke, there's fire.

On the back cover of Fred Kogos' From *Shmear* to Eternity *is a variation on a famous proverb:* Az sie brent, es a lox. *Where there's smoke, there's lox.*

Besser tsu shtarben shtai'endik aider tsu leben oif di k'ni.
Better to die upright than to live on your knees.

De länger ein Blinder lebt, desto mehr sieht er.
The longer a blind man lives, the more he sees.

Der mentsh trakht, un Got lakht.
*A man thinks and God laughs. (*The equivalent of the English phrase, *Man supposes and God disposes.)*

Der vos hot nit fazukht bitterreh, vaist nit voz zies iz.
One who has never tasted the bitter cannot know the sweet.

Der vos shveigt maint oikh epes.
He who is silent still means something.

Di epeleh falt nit veit fun baimeleh.
The apple doesn't fall far from the tree.

Di grub iz shoin ofen un der mensh tut nokh hofen.
The grave is already open and man still hopes.

Fahren dokter un aren beder zeinen nito kain soides.
There are no secrets from a doctor or a bathhouse attendant.

Fon ain oks tsit men akin tzvai fellen nit arop.
*You can't get two skins from one ox. (*There is a variation: *You can't sit on two chairs with one* tuches.)

Fon dein moil in Gotz oieren.
From your mouth to God's ears.

Fon kin'ah vert sin'ah.
Envy breeds hate.

Got hat eine welt voller kleiner weltchen ershaffen.
God created one world full of small worlds.

During the Holocaust, many Jews either joined with other partisan groups fighting against the Nazis or formed their own underground resistance groups. Their rallying cry was a song written by Hirsh Blik, with music by Dmitri Pokrass, called Zog Nit Keinmol, "Never Say." All Holocaust Memorial Day commemorations include, in Yiddish and English, the singing of "The Song of the Partisans":

Zog nit keyn mol az du geyst dem letsten veg,
Khotsh himlen blayene fahrsthtelen bloye teg.
Kumen vet nokh undzer oysgebenkte sha'ah,
S'vet a poyk ton undzer trot mir zaynen do!

Never say that you are going your last way,
Though lead-filled skies above blot out the blue of day.
The hour for which we long will certainly appear,
The earth shall thunder 'neath our tread that we are here!

Nit dos iz sheyn, vos iz sheyn, nor dos, vos es gefelt.
Beautiful is not what is beautiful, but what one likes.

Nit kain entfer iz oikh an entfler.
No answer is also an answer.

Oder es helft nit oder men darf es nit.
Either it doesn't help or you don't need it.

Oif vemens vogen me zitst, zingt men dem lied.
On whoever's wagon you're sitting, that's whose tune you're singing.

Reden iz shver un shveigen kenmen nit.
Speech is difficult, but silence impossible.

Reden iz zilber, shveigen iz gold.
Speech is silver, silence is golden.

Sheynkeit fahrgeit, khokhme bashteit.
Beauty fades, wisdom stays.

Ven me lakht ze'en alleh; ven me vaint zet kainer nisht.
When you laugh, all see; when you cry, no one sees.

Ven men darf hoben moi'akh, helft nit kain koi'akh.
When you need brains, brawn won't help.

Ven si fahrleshen zikh di likht, haiben on tasntsen di meiz.
When the lights go out, the mice dance. (When the cat's away, the mice will play.)

Ver filt zikh, der meynt zikh.
Who feels guilty, feels responsible.

Vos mer gevart, mer genart.
He who hesitates is lost.

Yeder hartz hot soides.
Every heart has secrets.

Yeder mensh iz oif zikh alain blind.
Every man is blind to his own faults.

CHAPTER THREE

Bei Mir Bist Du Shoen
It's All Yinglish to Me

In many ways, this book is about how to speak Yinglish, not Yiddish. Leo Rosten, author of *The Joys of Yiddish*, is credited with coining the word "Yinglish" to refer to an amalgam of English and Yiddish, a hybrid of English words given a Yiddish inflection, or Yiddish words given new meanings. Many native English speakers, including non-Jews, use Yinglish without being aware of it. Yinglish words can be heard daily, in common speech and in the mass media. The words have become so engrained into the English vernacular that, even though some may sound Yiddish, they are as much a part of standard English as any slang.

In addition, there are several words that Rosten dubbed "Ameridish," meaning they were used only in the United States. Many Yiddish language writers think "Yinglish" and "Ameridish" are synonymous because of the universal prevalence of U.S. television shows, not to mention the Internet. Some words listed below, however, are used only in the United States and others only in Great Britain.

There is also a third hybrid of Yiddish and English, specific to certain Orthodox communities, dubbed "Yeshivish." It is characterized by vocabulary, syntax, and inflections that combine both Yiddish and English. It is used by native English speakers who have picked up the "dialect" in the Jewish schools they attend. It differs from Yiddish in that the words are written in English characters, not Hebrew, and the Yiddish words are conjugated as though they were in English. The speech sounds like slightly eccentric or idiomatic standard English.

Listed below are just a few of the more colorful and familiar Yinglish words:

Fin
Five-dollar bill, from Yiddish *funf*, five.

I had to pay a *fin* to park for a quarter of an hour!

Futz
To fool around with, to mess with; has added advantage for teenagers of sounding like an expletive deleted. Its etymology is probably the Yiddish *arumfahrtsen*, to fart around.

Stop *futzing* around with the remote and find something to watch already.

Gazump
To cheat someone out of a property by bidding more than the previously accepted offer. The word is used in Britain and Australia to refer to a house purchase. Originally, it meant to swindle, which lends credence to the theory that the word comes from the Yiddish *gezumf*, to cheat or overcharge.

Gunsel.

In common usage, a hoodlum, armed gangster.

That bully down the street walks around with a Super Soaker and pretends he's a *gunsel*.

Although the word gunsel *is usually used to refer to a gunman, it originally meant a young homosexual hobo who was partners with an older tramp. It comes from the Yiddish* gentzl, *little goose. In* The Maltese Falcon, *when Sam Spade refers to Wilmer Cook as a* gunsel, *he is speaking of his sexual orientation and relationship with Kaspar Gutman, not his handgun.*

Ishkabbible

A dismissive statement: "Who cares?"

They're announcing the Grammy nominees today? *Ishkabbible*.

The word first appeared in a 1913 song, lyrics written by Sam M. Lewis and music by George W. Meyer, called "Isch Gabibble (I Should Worry)." The phrase has widely been considered to be Yiddish in origin, although there is no concensus as to its etymology. There are just as many linguists, however, who dismiss this contention, as the word "bibble," a cognate of "babble," appeared as early as the sixteenth century in Shakespeare's Twelfth Night: *"Endeavour thy selfe to sleepe, and leave thy vain bibble babble."*

Jalopy

An old, broken down car.

My son wants a new car, but I'd rather he drive a *jalopy* so we don't have to pay as much insurance.

It is possible the word comes from the Yiddish (which borrowed it from Polish) shlappe, an old horse. A more likely explanation is that the word comes from Jalapa, Mexico, where many used cars wound up.

Kibosh

To put the *kibosh* on something means to cancel it out, to dismiss it. It most likely comes from Yiddish, and the most plausible explanation is it comes from the Yiddish word *kabbastn*, to suppress.

My twelve-year-old wanted to go to an R-rated movie, but I put the *kibosh* on his plans.

Kokhalein

Literally, cook alone; figuratively a summer cottage with a kitchen, a bungalow. It comes from two Yiddish words *kokhn*, to cook, and *alein*, alone.

Every summer, my grandparents would get away from the hot city and stay at a *kokhalein* in the Catskills.

Mazoola, mazuma

Money. The word comes from the Yiddish *mezumen*, cash.

He'll even do something illegal, as long as he can make a lot of *mazoola*.

17

Ootz

Pester; tease or tweak; sometimes spelled "utz," but the word has nothing to do with a Pennsylvania Dutch brand of potato chips.

If you *ootz* the cat, she'll scratch you.

If we just *ootz* the proposal a bit more, we should be ready to send it out.

Shmegegge

Buffoon, idiot.

Do you know what that *shmegge* did? He went to an Eagles game in below freezing weather, and took off his shirt to show off his green chest.

Shmo

A nobody, a jerk.

He's not important, just a *Joe Shmo*.

Many Yiddishists believe the cartoonist Al Capp named his character the schmoo after the Yiddish word shmo. *The schmoo was a formless blob that would transform itself into any kind of food people wanted.*

Shnook

An ineffectual, dorky type, someone you can't take seriously.

I wouldn't hire him as a representative of the company. He's a nice guy, but such a *shnook* that he'd lose clients.

Shamus

A detective, comes from *shames*, a watchman.

I always liked Bogart better as *shamus* than a criminal.

Shemozzle

British slang for a quarrel, brawl, confusing situation or unfortunate plight, the word probably comes from *shlimazel*. The word is used in Ireland during the game of hurling (not to be confused with what fraternity brothers often do on Saturday nights).

I tried to watch the game on TV, but there was such a *shemozzle*, I turned it off.

Spiel

Glib talk, patter, from *shpeel*, the Yiddish word for play. *Shpeel* can be a verb, as in playing an instrument, or a noun, as in a skit. A Purim *shpeel* is a satirical play poking fun at anything and everything.

That salesman has a convincing *spiel*.

Yenemsville

Wherever, from the Yiddish *yenem*, someone else, whoever.

Our babysitter went back to college. But we don't want to replace her with just *yenem*. We'll need to find someone experienced.

We got lost looking for a shortcut and wound up in *Yenemsville*.

In addition, some suffixes can turn English words into Yiddishisms:

–meister

Literally, master, as in the English word quizmaster. For example, a *spinmeister* is Yinglish for spin-doctor, someone who can give a positive interpretation to a negative event. A *shlockmeister* is a purveyor of shoddy goods.

–nik

Originally from Russian (as in *Sputnik*), the Yiddish suffix *nik* indicates that a person or thing is associated with something else. *Alrightnik, nogoodnik, beatnik, peacenik* fall into this category, as well as *refusenik*, a Jew who was refused an exit visa from the Soviet Union. It is also used in modern Hebrew in the same way. *Seruvnik*, for example, is the Hebrew for *refusnik*; a *Hashomer Hatza'irnik* is a member of the Young Guard, a left-leaning Zionist youth group; and a *kibbutznik* is a member of a *kibbutz,* a collective farm.

A nudnik is a pest, as in "I told you, I don't like 'South Park.' Now stop making me to watch it. You're being a nudnik." It comes from the Yiddish nudyn, to bore. Alrightnik, a new immigrant who has done well for himself, comes from the Yinglish olreitnik and was used to refer to a smug upstart or braggard. A nogoodnik, a word first recorded in 1936, is the opposite of an alrightnik.

–chik

From the Slavic, to indicate a diminutive. The most familiar example to English speakers is *boychik*, often used as a term of affection.

Hey, *boychik*, how's it going?

–shm

Adding *shm* to the beginning of the second word makes it into an object of derision.

***Fancy shmancy.* I have seen more lavish birthday parties for two-year-olds.**

Another Yiddishism is the doubling of words. *Mishmash*, which comes from *gemish*, the Yiddish word for mixture, is an example of doubling, as is *pish-posh*, a word that sounds Yiddish but is not.

There are many people who think they can sound as though they're speaking in a Yiddish accent by using a New York one. The two accents are not the same. Fran Drescher does not have a Yiddish accent; Fannie Brice did. (Actually, she didn't, but she used one on stage. In fact, she didn't even speak Yiddish. You can hear the difference when Barbra Streisand, who played Fannie Brice in *Funny Girl* and *Funny Lady*, is doing one of Brice's acts and when she's portraying Brice's private life.) The classic Yiddish actress Molly Picon also had one only on stage; she normally spoke unaccented English. Mel Brooks has one as the *Two-Thousand-Year-Old Man* and as Yogurt in *Spaceballs*; he doesn't have one in *High Anxiety*. In *Crossing Delancey Street*, the grandmother has a Yiddish accent; the granddaughter does not. James Cagney, who wasn't Jewish but could speak fluent Yiddish, had a New York accent.

A Yiddish accent is heavily inflected with Russian or German or Polish cadences and pronunciations. If someone is banging on the front door, a native English speaker might say: "I'm coming already. Hold your horses." A native Yiddish speaker might say: "*Vas* is *der* matter? A fire, God forbid? I'll be dere fast as I can. You can vait maybe a minute?"

There are also certain sentence structures that make people sound as though they are speaking Yiddish rather than English. For example, it is a characteristic quirk of Yiddish to answer a question with a question: "How are you?" "*Nu*, how should I be?" Yiddish sentence structures include other syntactical devices, such as reversing the order of words ("A successful businessman, he is not.") or placing the emphasis in such a way as to indicate sarcasm or derision ("A *businessman* he thinks he is?")

21

The vocabulary sounds as though the words are translated from Yiddish into their literal English equivalents, rather than into colloquial or conversational English.

Fan of Star Wars *if you be, a Yiddish accent did not Yoda have, know you. But speak he did in sentence order reversed. Check out* http://www.yodaspeak.co.uk *to have more fun with Yoda.*

An example of literal translation can be seen in the use of "by" to mean "according to" or "with," as in "By you, a chiropractor is a doctor. By me, he's no doctor," or, "Don't worry about a babysitter. The children can stay by us."

The Andrews Sisters in their hit song "Bei Mir Bist Du Shoen" (using the German spelling), literally translated as "By Me You Are Beautiful," made use of "by" in this way. "Bei Mir Bist Du Schoen," written by Jacob Jacobs (lyrics) and Sholom Secunda (music) for a long-forgotten 1932 Yiddish musical, was rediscovered in 1937 by lyricist Sammy Cahn, who heard it at the Apollo Theater in Harlem—sung in Yiddish by an African-American duo named Johnnie and George. The audience—and Cahn—loved the song. He obtained the rights, rewrote it with Saul Chaplin using English lyrics, and convinced the Andrew Sisters, who were Lutheran, to record it later that year.

There are other words that are not Yiddish, but sound as though they could be.

Cockamamie

Inane, half-baked, silly

You're not painting your bedroom black. Wherever did you come up with such a *cockamamie* idea?

According to many etymological dictionaries, the word "cockamamie" comes from decalcomania, a fad in the 1840s in France and later in England, of decorating furniture—and skin—with decals. It has had a revival more recently as decoupage and temporary tattoos.

Compote

A stew made of dried fruits such as apricots and prunes. The word is not Yiddish, but most Eastern European languages have cognates that mean the same thing.

We always have *compote* on Passover to counteract the effects of too much *matzo*.

Kitsch

From the German word for "gaudy," which is why it sounds Yiddish.

She thinks she has good taste, but those earrings are *kitschy*.

Potrzebie

A made up word scattered throughout *Mad Magazine*. The story is that editor Harvey Kurtzman saw the Polish word *potrzeba*, meaning needed or necessity, and decided it would make a great nonsense word. It first appeared in the April, 1954, letters column. Someone asked for the the meaning of *furshlugginer,* and the answer was, "It means the same as *"potrzebie."*

My son's such a smart aleck. I asked him what he wants for his birthday, and he said, "A brand new *potrzebie.*"

Mad Magazine *is filled with words that are either Yiddish (ganef, fahrshluggine, fahrshimelt, shmendrick) or sound as though they could be (veeblefetzer, feh, ech, shmeck, hoo ha). The writers used Yiddishisms for some of their great puns, like a take off of "Mandrake the Magician" called "Shmendrake the Magician," and a spin on the "I Like Ike" electioneering slogan: "I Like Lox."*

Shyster

A shady or dishonest lawyer.

He might be a *shyster,* but he always gets his clients off.

Although often referring to Jewish lawyers, the term shyster *is used for any lawyer who is not quite kosher. The word comes from* sheis, *the German word for shit, a rather appropriate etymology. The word may also be connected to Shylock, although Shakespeare's character was a moneylender, not a lawyer. The only lawyer in the play was Portia, whose name has become synonymous with "woman lawyer." Whether she was a shyster is a matter of interpretation and perspective.*

CHAPTER FOUR

Iz Nisht Kosher

Words Familiar to English Speakers

Just as Yiddish-speakers who moved to English-speaking countries incorporated English words into Yiddish, so too did Yiddish words gradually become part of casual English vocabulary. In a reciprocal cultural exchange, non-Jewish English speakers now use many Yiddish words, sometimes without realizing their etymologies. Listen to the radio, go to a movie or play, watch a TV show, surf the Internet, eavesdrop on a casual conversation, and you will hear Yiddish.

It doesn't seem to matter whether the speaker is from a metropolitan area with a large Jewish population or from an isolated rural community, certain Yiddish words have become standard English. Many are even recognized by word processing programs as being spelled correctly. (Ones that are not accepted can lead to some amusing suggestions: "slipper" for *shlepper*, for example, "bubbles" for *bubkes*, "gaunt" for *gezunt*, its exact opposite.) Kosher (as in "That deal doesn't sound quite kosher to me."); *chutzpah* (classic definition: A man kills his parents and asks the judge for mercy because he's an orphan); *shlep* ("I can't believe my boss wants me to shlep all the way across town during rush hour to pick up a file that could be e-mailed;" or "How did you manage to shlep all those grocery bags up three flights of stairs?"); the derogatory *shlemiel* ("She had the chutzpah to try and fix me up with that shlemiel") and the vulgarisms *shmuck*, *putz*, and *drek* have all made their way into English slang.

Bubkes
Nothing.

I play the Lottery every week, and what do I get? *Bubkes*.

Chutzpah
Refers to nerve and guts, but not in the sense of physical bravery so much as impudence and arrogance; the idea that one can get away with anything.

He got a D– on his essay and then had the *chutzpah* **to criticize mine.**

Fahrshtaits.
Understand.

I'm tired of repeating myself, so listen carefully.
Fahrshtaits?

Fumfn.
To mumble, search for right word, also transliterated as *fonfn*.

He's a terrible public speaker. All he does is *fumfn*.

I can't believe Marlon Brando got such good reviews for
The Godfather. **I couldn't understand a word he said. All he did was** *fonfn*.

Gezunt, Gezuntehait.
Health.

Abi gezunt—dos lebn ken men zikh alain nemen.
Be well—you can kill yourself later.

Gai gezunt.
Go in health.

Gai gezuntehait.
Have a good trip. Go in good health.

Gai gezunt un kum gezunt.
Go in health and come in health.

Gai gezunt un kum gezunt.
Have a wonderful vacation.

Ghetto
The origin of the word—and the concept and the reality—is Italian, as Venice had the first *ghetto*. It referred originally to a segregated neighborhood where Jews were required to reside, but is now is used for any restricted neighborhood, whether *de jure* (as in Apartheid-era South Africa) or *de facto* (as in the Gilded *Ghettos* where many affluent Americans live).

Beverly Hills is a Gilded *Ghetto*.

Glitch
From the Yiddish word for "smooth, slippery," a *glitch* is when something has gone wrong, in the sense of "slipped up."

Whenever he messes up on the computer, he says there's a *glitch* in the software.

Hamish
Either a Scottish first name or the Yiddish word for a place that is welcoming, comfortable, and home-like.

The members of that small synagogue think they've created a *hamish* environment, but they're all a bunch of nudniks and busybodies.

Klutz

Someone who is clumsy, a person who always trips or drops things. Not as out of control as a bull in a china shop, but you don't want to serve them dinner on your best dishes.

My sister is such a *klutz*. I think I'll use paper plates tonight.

Kosher

The word to describe foods that conform to Jewish dietary laws literally means "proper, legal," and refers to anything honest and above-board. Watch any British crime show, and you are sure to hear the word.

Our neighbor is selling DVDs really cheap. I'm not sure they're *kosher*.

Kosher *foods do not mix dairy and meat at the same meal. This has led to several categories of foods:* flaishik *(meat);* milchik *(dairy);* pareve *(neutral; also spelled* parve*);* glatt *(from the word for "smooth," refers to unblemished lungs in a cow, and is used colloquially as "super* Kosher*");* Pesadikh *(Kosher for Passover); and, of course,* traif *(non-Kosher food). The most* traifedika *sandwich I can think of is ham and cheese with butter on white bread.*

Kvell

To be proud of.

They *kvell* whenever their *kindelakh* do anything, even if it's unremarkable.

Kvetch

To complain.

You can't go swimming during a thunderstorm and *kvetching* about it will not make a difference.

L'Chaim

As anyone who has seen *Fiddler on the Roof* knows, *L'chaim* means "To life." It is a toast in Hebrew, Yiddish, and, increasingly, English. It can also be used ironically.

So, you got away with cheating on the test? *L'chaim*.

Mazel tov

Congratulations. (It can be used ironically.)

So, you finally decided to come visit your mother? *Mazel tov*!

Mitzvah

Something that has been commanded by God, a religious requirement or obligation. Used generally to refer to a good deed.

My daughter would be doing a real *mitzvah* if she'd clean up her room. It will keep me from killing her.

Makhen a mitzvah

To do a good deed; a euphemism for having sex (usually within marriage).

Nu

An untranslatable interjection, similar to "So?"

Your landlord is increasing your rent? *Nu*, what do you plan to do now?

Plotz

Literally, to explode, but not in the sense of anger. It has a connotation of collapsing.

I am about to *plotz* from all the work I have to do.

Pogrom

Officially sanctioned riots, rampages, murders, rapes, and arsons perpetrated by anti-Semites against the Jews living in *shtetls* (small towns), large cities, ghettos, or anywhere else they resided and were persecuted.

If my great-great grandparents hadn't left Ukraine for the United States after the 1903 *pogrom* in Kishinev, our family might have perished in the Holocaust.

In April 1903, on Easter weekend in Kishinev, then the capital of Bessarabia and now of Moldavia, forty-nine Jews were killed, almost six hundred were wounded, and over seven hundred houses looted and destroyed during a pogrom. It was instigated by rumors published in local newspapers that the Jews had murdered a Christian boy in order to use his blood to make matzo. Such accusations are called blood libels. They disregard the fact that Jewish dietary laws prohibit the eating of any blood, and to be considered kosher, animals must be salted and soaked in order to ensure that no blood remains. They also ignore the importance of the Sixth

Commandment forbidding murder. In April 2008, posters appeared in Novosibirsk, the third largest city in Russia, warning parents about the approach of Passover: "These vermin [Jews] are still performing rituals, stealing small children and draining their blood to make their sacred bread."

Shlep

To drag around.

My mother made me *shlep* her all over town looking for a blouse to match a skirt that didn't look good on her anyway.

A *shlepper* can be a gofer, but he can also be someone who lacks ambition, is a hanger-on.

According to Hollywood, if you're bright and get a job as a *shlepper* in a warehouse, you'll eventually marry the boss's daughter and take over the company.

She married a real *shlepper*. He always has excuses for not finding a job.

The adjective *shleppy* describes someone who is disheveled, slovenly.

Put on a clean shirt. You look *shleppy*.

Shlock

Cheaply made goods. Also used for bad or trashy entertainment.

I can't believe you spent good money for that *shlock*.

Why are you watching that *shlock*? Put on PBS instead.

Shmooze

Similar to *kibitz*, but more in the sense of aimless chatting than gossiping.

Forget about "If you snooze, you lose." In this job, if you *shmooze*, you lose.

Shabbos

Sabbath, the Day of Rest, from sundown Friday night until sundown Saturday.

He says he observes *Shabbos*, but I saw him pull into a Dunkin' Donuts on the way home from shul.

Traditionally observant Jews refrain from doing work, including cooking, driving, or using electricity, which includes turning lights on and off. Some tear toilet paper before Shabbos begins, and unscrew the bulb in the refrigerator so it does not turn on when the door is opened. In order to turn lights on and off either at home or in the synagogue, a non-Jew would be hired to do those tasks. This person was called a Shabbos goy.

Shabbos goy

A non-Jew hired to do the tasks forbidden on the Sabbath.

The synagogue president insisted they hire a *Shabbos goy* to open up and close the *shul*.

There are several famous men who were Shabbos goys when they were young. Elvis Presley was so happy to help Rabbi Albert Fruchter of Memphis keep Shabbos that he refused to accept any money from him.

General Colin Powell, who grew up in the South Bronx and spoke Yiddish, earned a quarter for turning the lights on and off in an Orthodox synagogue on Friday nights. And former New York governor Mario Cuomo has said of his parents' friends the Kesslers, "I was a Shabbos goy *because of them." When both Al Gore and Joe Lieberman were in the Senate together, Gore acted as Lieberman's* Shabbos goy. *When Lieberman would stay overnight in his office so he could cast votes on* Shabbos, *Gore would come in to turn the lights on and off for him.*

Shmutz

Dirt. Can refer to physical or metaphorical dirt.

Who tracked that *shmutz* onto my clean floor?

I don't care if they do publish literary articles. Playboy is still *shmutzik*.

Shrek, shreklikh

Horror, a fright. Not to be confused with shriek, although a *shrek* can cause you to do so. Also not to be confused with the anti-Disney character of the same name, whose creators undoubtedly were familiar with the Yiddish word.

My teenaged son's room is *shreklikh*. It's a health hazard.

Shtick

A piece. The word is sometimes spelled *shtik*, but computer programs do not recognize that spelling.

She's fooled herself into thinking that if she breaks up the candy bar into *shticks*, there won't be as many calories. No wonder she keeps gaining weight.

In English, *shtick* often refers to a particular trait or mannerism.

I know it's just her *shtick*, but it drives me crazy when she always has to hug everyone.

It can refer to a stand-up comedian's act or an actor's typical role.

Owen Wilson always plays the same kind of slightly goofy, sensitive male character. It's his *shtick*.

The suffix –l or –el transforms a noun into a diminutive. The addition of –leh makes the word into a superdiminutive. For example, a shtikl *is a small piece of something and a* shtikeleh *is even smaller.*

Shtumm
Silence. Used quite often in British movies and television shows.

Stay *shtumm* and maybe Mom won't notice we broke the dish.

Shul
Synagogue. From the German word for school, as a synagogue is also a place of study.

We go to *shul* religiously.

Shvitz
A steam bath.

My grandfather used to go out on Thursday nights with "the boys" to sit in the *shvitz*, smoke cigars, play pinochle, and *shmooze*. It was the highlight of his week.

As a verb, it means to sweat.

The air conditioning is broken and I can't stop *shvitzing*.

A *shvitzer* is not necessarily someone who is perspiration challenged, but a braggart.

That *shvitzer* I work with had to make sure everyone knew he got a new sportscar.

Tchotchke
Bauble, worthless item, a dust catcher.

My Enterprise Christmas ornament is not a *tchotchke*. It's a rare and valuable Star Trek collectible.

Tsuris
Trouble.

First she lost her job, then her dog died, and now she has the flu. I have never seen one person have so much *tsuris* all at once.

Yeshiva
Generally, a religious school for advanced study. Also the name of a Jewish university in New York City. A young man who attends a traditional yeshiva is a *yeshiva bokher* (yeshiva boy or bachelor).

He's a *yeshiva bokher*, so he'll need to find a wife who will be able to support the family.

CHAPTER FIVE

Vi Iz Ayer Nomen?

What's in a Name?

There's an old bilingual joke. (To understand it, you need to know the Yiddish words *fahrgessen* means "forgotten" and *shoyn* means "already.") A recently arrived Jewish immigrant from Eastern Europe settled on the Lower East Side of New York and introduced himself to his neighbors as Sean Fergusson. "Sean Fegusson?" one exclaimed. "What kind of name is that for a nice Jewish boy?" The man explained: "I met a helpful man on the ship. He asked me my name and I told him. He said, 'You can't go to America with a name like that. You need a simple American name. Tell them your name is John Smith.' When I got to shore and the official asked me my name, I said, '*Shoyn fergessen.*' That's what he wrote down."

It's widely believed that the immigration officials at Ellis Island changed Jewish names to be more Anglo-sounding. In actuality, the officials copied the names directly from the ships' manifests, which were compiled at the point of embarkation. The name changes, therefore, were made either by shipping officials in Europe or by the families themselves before they bought their tickets.

Many Jews later Anglicized their names, and not just to assimilate. For example, many a Fox was born Fuchs (pronounced *fyooks*), but changed the name so as to avoid the inevitable mispronunciation and subsequent teasing. But others, particularly those in show business, did change their names so they would be more "acceptable" to *goyishe* America.

Not every actor changed to a more "American"-sounding name. Tovah Feldshuh, for example, was born Terri Sue. For a while she acted under the name Terri Fairchild, but then decided to use her Hebrew name.

Originally, Jews did not have surnames, but were known by patronymics. Dovid, whose father's name was Shmuel, was called Dovid ben Shmuel. In English, his name would be David Samuelson.

In 1787, the Austrian Empire issued a decree ordering Jews to register with surnames taken from the German language. In 1808, Napoleon decreed that Jews adopt fixed names, to assist with census taking and tax collection. Similar laws were passed in Prussia in 1812, Poland in 1821, and Russia in 1844.

According to some sources (but not substantiated in others), Jews had to pay a registration fee, and those who could not afford to pay were assigned offensive or derogatory names, while the wealthy would be given pleasant names, like Rosenfeld (field of roses). The name Spater (later) was often given to Jews who were late in registering.

Most names were patronymics (Shuelovitz—Saul's son), occupations (Schneider—tailor), hometowns (Litwack—one from Lithuania), or physical characteristics (Klein—small). But whether or not it is true that officials gave silly-sounding names to the poor, those names can be found in many lists, even if they are no longer in use. Among them are:

- Affengesicht (monkey face)
- Dreyfus (third foot, euphemism for penis)
- Harn (urine)
- Kaker (crapper)
- Stinker (bad smelling)
- Schlanger (from *shlong*, euphemism for penis)
- Langnuz (long nose)

Fictional Names

Authors sometimes give their Jewish characters names that are vulgar, coarse or insulting, usually used for comedic effect. Although when Shakespeare named his character Shylock in *The Merchant of Venice*, the name was not yet a synonym for usurer, but was in use with that meaning within a century.

In his 1896 novel, *Leib Weihnachtskuchen and His Child*, set in Galicia, author Karl Emil Franzos named his protagonist *Weihnachtskuchen*, Christmas Cake.

In contemporary times, Woody Allen's stories, especially the later ones, contain names, many in English, which broadcast a character's personality or occupation; for example, Wiseman for a rabbi, Peplum for a tailor, or Fleshpot for a *femme fatale*. Others of Allen's surnames are Yiddish (or Yiddish-sounding) words, also used for satirical purposes. Among them are Bidnik, Eppis, Goldworm, Kugelmass, Mandelstam, Pinchuk, Schmeed, Schmeederer, Sheigitz, Untermensch, Varnishke, and Zipsky.

Several fictional names (some from published works) became part of colloquial Yiddish. Most of them refer to fools:

Chaim Yankel
A fool, a bumpkin

Chelmner
The fictional residents of the real Polish town of Chelm were known as the epitome of foolishness. Stories about "the wisemen of Chelm" are still popular folktales.

Kuni Lemel
An ineffectual fool, made famous in a series of eponymous plays and Israeli movies (*The Two Kuni Lemel, Kuni Lemel in Tel Aviv, Kuni Lemel in Cairo*)

Moishe Kapoyer
One who does everything backwards; created by humor columnist B. Kovner for the *Forverts*.

Moishe Pupik
Someone with an exaggerated and unwarranted image of himself; the name may have evolved from a nickname for an actual man named Moishe who had a large stomach and larger ego.

Moishe Zugmir
Literally, "Moses Tell-Me;" figuratively, "John Doe" or "Whatshisname?

CHAPTER SIX

Freg Mikh B'Kherem

Outside the Pale

"I look upon you, sir, as a man who has placed himself beyond the pale of society, by his most audacious, disgraceful, and abominable public conduct."—The Pickwick Papers, *Charles Dickens, 1837.*

In 1791, Catherine the Great established the Pale of Settlement as the area of Russia in which Jews were allowed to live. Comprising twenty percent of European Russia and located on its western side stretching to Central Europe, the Pale roughly corresponded to the modern borders of Lithuania, Poland, Ukraine, Moldavia, Belarus, and parts of western Russia. Ninety percent of Russian Jews resided within the Pale. Not only were they subject to discrimination and restrictions, being taxed at a higher rate and forbidden from owning land, but also the high concentration of their population in a limited space made them more easily subject to pogroms. Under the May Laws of 1882, they were further restricted to urban areas only.

Not coincidentally, it was around this time that Jewish emigration to the United States increased dramatically, with an estimated two million settling in the United States from 1881 to 1914.

The phrase "outside the Pale" refers to an area outside of which local laws do not apply. Figuratively, "outside the Pale" has come to refer to the Other, to anyone who is not part of the normative community standards of behavior or belief. Despite popular thought, the etymology of the phrase "outside the Pale" most likely comes not from the Jewish Pale of Settlement in Russia but from the English Pale in Ireland, an area of the island that came under the direct influence of England from the thirteenth to the sixteenth centuries.

What They Call Us

Anti-Semitism is not manifested only through pogroms. Offensive words broadcast hatred as much as physical violence.

- *Christ Killer:* It was not until the Second Vatican Council in 1965 that the Jews were officially absolved of responsibility for the Crucifixion. The expression, however, is still heard, and the sentiment behind it is still existent.
- *Four Wheel:* The phrase is British, and comes from Cockney rhyming slang: "four wheel skid" is colloquial for *Yid*.
- *Hymie:* A disparaging name when used by goyim, unless it is someone's nickname. It comes from the Hebrew name *Chaim*, often Anglicized as *Hyman*.
- *Kike:* Probably the best-known odious name, the word comes from *keikl*, the Yiddish word for circle. There are several different theories about its etymology:
  - In medieval Germany, Jews were required to wear a yellow circle on the shoulder of their coats.
  - New immigrants to the United States who were mentally deficient had a chalk circle drawn on their clothing.

- Jewish immigrants to the United States who did not know how to write their names in English signed with a circle instead of an X, which reminded them of a cross.
- According to the *Oxford English Dictionary*, the etymology of the word is the commonly used suffixes –(s)ky or––(s)ki in Jewish surnames.
- Pope Clement VIII (1536–1605) denounced the "blind (*caeca* in Latin) obstinacy" of the Jews.
- Jewish clothing manufacturers were accused of making cheap copies of haute couture after having "peeped" at the designs. The German word "to peep" is *kieken.*
- The term may be an acronym for "Christ Killer" (K.K.)
- *Sheeny:* The etymology is unknown, but the word may come from the Yiddish *shayne*, beautiful. Jews often use the adjective, sometimes admiringly and sometimes ironically.

Such a *shaine maidl* (pretty girl) should have no problem getting a date for the prom.

Hey, *shaine punim* (beautiful face), stop futzing around with your hair and get to work.

Henry Ford was a noted anti-Semite. To this day, there are many Jews who will not buy Ford automobiles because of his beliefs. This is a popular joke based on Ford's views: The three Goldberg brothers, Norman, Hyman, and Max invented the first automobile air conditioner. They visited Ford and convinced him to come out to their car. It was a hot day, and the inside of the car was even hotter. When they turned on the air conditioner, the car cooled off immediately.

Ford offered them three million dollars for the patent. They said they would settle for two million, but only if they received recognition by having the label "The Goldberg Air Conditioner" affixed to the dashboard of every car in which it was installed. There was no way Ford was going to agree to having the Jewish name Goldberg emblazoned on two million cars that carried the Ford name. After hours of negotiations, it was agreed that Ford would pay them four million dollars for the patent and that just their first names would be shown.

And that is why, even today, all Ford air-conditioners show on the controls, the names "Norm, Hi, & Max."

What We Call Them

Unfortunately, victims of bigotry can also be prejudiced. Yiddish has many derogatory words for anyone who is not Jewish.

Golakh

A monk. It means "smooth" and refers to the tonsure.

Goy

From the Hebrew word for "nation," a *goy* is any non-Jew. The word is not always used only as a description or as a compliment.

What can you expect from the *goyim?*

Goyishe kop

Literally, a gentile head. It is not a description of someone with straight blonde hair and a small nose. It refers to someone who lacks common sense and is not too bright.

She sent out her resume without proofreading, and it was full of typos. What do you expect from a *goyishe kop*?

Nitelnacht

Literally, "birth night"; Yiddish word for Christmas Eve; related to "natal." Because Jews do not believe the Messiah ("Christ" in Greek; *moshiakh* in Yiddish) has arrived, they avoid Yiddish words that would imply that he has.

Jews traditionally celebrate *Nitelnacht* by going out for Chinese food and a movie.

Shaigitz

The word for non-Jewish man. Unlike the word *shiksa,* which can sometimes be a compliment, *shaigitz* is always used disparagingly. It has a connotation of someone who is lower class, unsophisticated, uneducated. The plural is *shkotzim,* a word that sounds as disdainful as it means. A *shkutz* is a boor. The word comes from the Hebrew, in the Book of Genesis, for creepy crawlies.

It was bad enough she married a non-Jew, but she had to go marry a *shaigitz* who grew up in a trailer park.

The *shkutz* next door sits on his front steps drinking beer in his undershirt.

Shiksa

A non-Jewish woman. The word can be used derisively or admiringly.

I have to admit she is a good wife to him. I just wish she weren't a *shiksa*.

The blonde *shiksa* goddess is the dream of every Jewish *nebbish* from Philip Roth to Woody Allen to Ben Stiller.

Shvartze

Black. Well before coloreds became blacks, Jews called African-Americans *shvartzes*. The word was used descriptively, not pejoratively. It is the word for the color black. Nevertheless, it is seldom heard these days, as some think of it as being a derogatory or offensive word.

She's got such a tan she looks like a *shvartze*.

My great-great grandfather had black hair, so he was named Schwartz.

Often, it referred to the janitor in an apartment building or a cleaning woman.

Don't try to fix the light yourself. Let the *shvartze* do it.

It could also refer to a calamity, as in the English expression "It is a black day."

Last year was *a shvartz yor af mir* (a bad year for me). I was diagnosed with cancer. But *barukh hashem* (Thank God), I am fine now.

Sylvesternacht; Sylvester

Literally, Sylvester's Eve; refers to New Year's Eve. Because the holiday of Rosh Hashanah begins the Jewish year, and December 31 in the Church calendar is dedicated to Saint Sylvester, Jews in Israel still call the secular New Year's Day Sylvester.

Our best friends are having a party for *Sylvesternacht*.

Yishka

Little Jesus, diminutive form of Yishu, Jesus, used to emphasize his Jewish birth while diminishing his importance.

What We Call Ourselves

Jews are just as hard on themselves as non-Jews. But, as with any group, we can call each other names that would be anti-Semitic if said by a non-Jew.

In the insular and isolated world of the *shtetl,* to become non-observant was almost as bad as converting to Christianity.

In the United States today, there are many "flavors" of Judaism. Traditional Jews alone can be divided into Orthodox, Modern Orthodox, and Chasidic, with several Chasidic sects, each following the teachings of a different rabbinic authority. Other movements, official or not, are Conservadox (more traditional than Conservative but not as much as Orthodox), Conservative, Reconstructionist, Reform, Renewal, Secular, and Humanistic.

Although the Reform and Conservative movements began in the mid-nineteenth century in Germany, they flourished in the United States. In Eastern Europe, there were really only two choices: to be observant or secular. There were no shades of gray. You were either observant or non-observant.

In the eighteenth century, there was a new, revolutionary movement in the Jewish world of Eastern Europe: the Chasidim. Founded by the Ba'al Shem Tov (the Master of the Good Name), the movement emphasized joyous, spiritual, spontaneous prayer and observance, rather than the dry legalistic pieties of the scholarly rabbinic authorities in the *Yeshivas* of the day. The Ba'al Shem Tov taught that even the uneducated had the ear of God, and that one did not have to be a *yeshiva bokher* to experience God. The holders of the status quo, the leaders of the *Yeshivas*, were called *Misnagdim*, opponents. It is ironic that the Chasidim are now regarded as the most stringent of traditional Jews. But they still believe in singing and dancing as paths to God.

The two groups ceased their animosity in the face of a common enemy: *haskalah*, the Enlightenment. The *haskalah*, beginning in the late eighteenth century in Germany, marked a movement toward increasing contacts between the Jewish communities and the "outside" world. It led the way toward secularization and the development of more liberal religious movements.

Apikoros

A heretic.

What do you mean you want to study Spinoza? He was an *apikoros*.

Kherem

Excommunication.

What are you doing? If the anyone sees you smoking on *Shabbos*, you'll be in *kherem*.

Freg mikh b'kherem.

Ask me in kherem; *in other words,* how should I know?

~~~~~~~~~~~~~~~~~~~~~~~~~~~~~~~~~~~~~~~

The most famous person to be placed in kherem *was the philosopher Baruch Spinoza, because of his rationalistic philosophy and enlightened approach to the Bible.* Kherem *was a very real threat to a Jew in the* shtetl. *He could be part of no community at all if shunned by other Jews. Unless the person in* kherem *converted to Christianity, there would be no acceptance by the general population either. Today,* kherem *is not a threat except to the most Orthodox. In 1945, Rabbi Mordecai M. Kaplan, the founder of Reconstructionist Judaism, was placed in* kherem *by the Union of Orthodox Rabbis, following the*

publication of Kaplan's new prayer book, which rejected the supernaturalism of God and the chosenness of the Jewish people. Afterwards, Kaplan often commented that since he did not belong to the same denomination as the rabbis of the Union of Orthodox Rabbis, their excommunication was meaningless.

Oysvorf

Literally, an outcast, a scoundrel, a nonconformist.

If you keep talking like an *apikoros*, you'll be an *oysvorf*.

Shaigets einer

Literally, a true non-Jew; refers to an irreligious Jew.

I heard that *shaigets einer* eats pork—and on Yom Kippur no less!

Traifener kop

Literally, a non-*Kosher* head, the phrase refers to a non-observant Jew.

That *traifener kop* hasn't stepped inside a synagogue since he turned thirteen.

Someone who comes from the same area as you is a *landsman*, a countryman. *Landsmen* banded together in the United States to help one another become acclimated to the *Goldene Medina* (the Golden State—not California, but the United States). Their organizations, called *landsmanshaften*, gave financial aid and advice to the *greeners* (green horns) who quickly discovered that the streets were paved with cobblestones, mud, and horseshit, not gold. Anyone who came from the same area was automatically a *landsman*. Anyone else was considered inferior. The following words have two meanings. For those who came from these places, they were a badge of pride; for others, a term of derision.

Ashkenazi

All Jews of Central or Eastern European descent, as opposed to the Sephardim, those who trace their roots to the Iberian peninsula pre-1492. Ashkenazim consider Sephardim to be uncultured shepherds and Sephardim consider Ashkenazim to be uncultured religious fanatics. As with any stereotypes, both are right and both are wrong.

Galitzianer

Galitzia was the section of Eastern Europe that was part of the Austro-Hungarian Empire from 1772, when it was partitioned from Poland, until the end of World War I, when it was ceded back to the newly reestablished state of Poland. In 1945, it was divided between Poland, controlled by the Soviet Union, and Ukraine, occupied by the Soviets. After the fall of the Soviet system, Ukraine and Poland became independent again. Galitzianers were considered inferior by the Litvaks, who thought of them as boorish and sentimental.

Litvak

Litvaks came from the area around Lithuania and Latvia. Borders being fluid, people from current day Russia, Poland, Belarus and other countries were Litvaks. Litvaks were considered inferior by Galitzianers, who thought of them as humorless and doctrinaire.

Vos-Vos

A derogatory term in popular use after World War II for a Yiddish speaker, used by those who did not speak Yiddish, such as Israelis or assimilated English-speakers. It comes from such Yiddish expressions as *Fahr vos*? ("What for?") or *Vos iz dokh?* ("What is that?").

Yekke

If there is one thing Galitizianers and Litvaks can agree on, it is that no one likes *Yekkes*. They are the upper class, assimilated German Jews who have adopted the German characteristics of frugality, cleanliness, and inflexibility. They were the WASPS of the Jewish world.

Yid

Literally, Jew. Used by non-Jews in a derogatory manner, but descriptively by Jews. *Yiddishkeit* means Jewishness in all its manifestations, particularly cultural.

Vos macht a yid?

What does a Jew make? Colloquial for *"How are you?" "What are you up to?"* The same grammatical construction as the German *Was machst du*? for *"How's it going?"*

They are not observant, but they still have that *pintele Yid* (point of light, spark of Jewishness) and there's a lot of *Yiddishkeit* in their home.

Yiddene

Literally, a Jewish woman; figuratively, a wife

She's such a good *Yiddene*, you'd never know she is a convert.

CHAPTER SEVEN

Shtadlans and Shnorrers

The Public Sphere

Life for Jews in Eastern Europe was far from easy. They were often prohibited from owning land and could enter only certain professions, commerce and banking among them. It is no surprise then that there were two public arenas in which Jews were active: socialist politics and business. When they came to the United States, many of the Jewish new immigrants entered business, either as workers in sweatshops or as purveyors of goods sold from pushcarts. Those who worked in the sweatshops often were also active in union politics and socialist political movements.

One is a lie, two is a lie, three is politics.
Ainer iz a ligen, tzvai iz ligens, drei iz politik.

The Russian Tsar and the Austrian Kaiser were the ultimate deciders of the Jews' fate in Central and Eastern Europe, but it was the petty official that the Jewish community had to deal with on a day-to-day basis. Many political organizations, generally underground ones, sprang up in the Jewish urban centers, and often fought with each other as much as they fought the establishment. Members of the Bund, a secular socialist party dedicated to establishing democratic socialism in Russia, were philosophically and politically in opposition to the Zionists, whom they believed were running away from the problems of the *golus* (Diaspora). The Zionists, who believed they were solving the problems of the *golus* by establishing a Jewish state, were divided into Labor Zionists, Religious Zionists, Revisionist Zionists, Cultural Zionists, and pocketbook Zionists (those who supported the idea of a Jewish state with donations rather than actions). Thus the saying, "Two Jews, three opinions."

Arbeiter Ring

Workman's Circle, a socialist-leaning philanthropic, cultural, political, social, and educational organization that helped immigrant Jews to maintain their ethnic identity while acclimating to American life.

My grandparents were not religious, so they sent my father to the *Arbeiter Ring* to learn about Jewish culture and Yiddish literature instead of to Hebrew School where he would have learned about religious laws and how to pray in Hebrew.

In addition to being involved with union organizing, the Workman's Circle ran (and in some communities, still runs) English language classes for adults, afternoon and summer programs for school children, and credit unions. The Folksbeine Playhouse, the oldest Yiddish theater still in existence, established in 1915, is run by the Workman's Circle in New York, and offers both classic and modern Yiddish productions.

The I. L. Peretz School network runs almost a dozen community, secular Jewish schools throughout the country, dedicated to keeping alive the culture of the Eastern European Jewish communities. The schools offer language (Hebrew as well as Yiddish), history, song, dance, art, music, and holiday celebrations. The Workman's Circle magazine, Jewish Currents, *is published in English. You can order a Sholem Aleichem bobblehead from their website.*

Borzhvaz; Borzhvazee

Bourgeois; bourgeoisie; middle class property-owning conformists and capitalists.

My grandfather was involved with the Socialist Party and was ashamed when my father bought a house in the suburbs and became a *borzhvaz*.

Fahrbrent.

Literally, burning; refers to someone who is zealous.

My great grandmother was a *fahrbrente* suffragette.

Freidenker.

Freethinker; atheist, secularist.

My grandparents almost sat *shiva* (seven days of mourning following a death) when my aunt announced she would not go to *shul* any longer because she was a *freidenker*.

Kapore

Scapegoat.

Every time there was a problem, the government made the Jews into the *kapore*.

Kemfer

Fighter, activist.

After the Triangle Shirtwaist Factory fire, my great grandfather became a *kemfer* for the unions.

On March 25, 1911, 146 mostly young, Jewish immigrant women were killed when fire broke out in the Triangle Shirtwaist Factory. The workers, some as young as twelve, worked long hours and earned about $7.00 a week. The average age of the victims was nineteen. The owners of the Triangle, Isaac Harris and Max Blanck, were tried for manslaughter but were acquitted. They were later sued in civil court and ordered to pay $75.00 in compensation for each victim. In the wake of the fire, the ILGWU—and labor unions in general—gained more support for their position and pushed for workplace safety legislation and workman's compensation. The building now houses the Chemistry Department of New York University and it is on the National Register of Historic Places.

Khopper

A kidnapper who took the sons of poor Jews to be conscripted into the Russian army for twenty-five years; from the Yiddish word for grabber. Those kidnapped were called *cantonistas*, referring to the districts (cantons) where their barracks were located.

My great-great grandparents sent my great grandfather to the United States to escape the *khoppers*.

Khaver

Comrade; used in modern Hebrew for a member of a *kibbutz,* a pal, or a boyfriend.

He was my great uncle's *khaver* in the union movement.

Shohad

Bribe.

When my cousin was on trial for embezzlement, he tried to give a juror a *shohad*.

Shtadlan

Court Jew, a factotum who had influence with the rulers and could intercede for the Jewish community. Generally, the *shtadlan* was a banker who lent money to the Christian upper classes.Sometimes a term of derision for a sell-out, someone who compromised his principles or toadied up to authority.

The *shtadlan* might think the duke is his friend, but the duke hates him even more than he hates the rest of the Jews, because he owes him a debt.

A good livelihood cures all ills.
Parnosseh iz a refueh tzu alleh krenk.

Many Jews who sold goods from pushcarts aspired to "move indoors" and open a store. Jews established many large department stores, some of which are still in business.

A Quaker from Nantucket named Rowland H. Macy established Macy's in the 1860s. After his death a decade later, the Straus brothers, sons of a German

> *Jewish peddler, purchased the store. (One of the broth-*
> *ers, Isador, later perished on the Titanic along with his*
> *wife, who refused to leave the ship without him.) Among*
> *other German Jewish families who founded department*
> *stores were the Altmans, Gimbels, Filenes, Magnins,*
> *Kaufmanns, Siegels, Lazaruses, Goldwaters, and Mays.*

From the words having to do with commerce, one could get the misleading impression not only that Jews were obsessed by money, but that they also used unethical practices in their business dealings, always trying to better the competition, even if they had to resort to underhanded methods to succeed.

A groys gesheft zol er hobn mit shroyre: vus er hot, zol men bay im nit fregn, un vos men fregt zol er nisht hobn.
He should have a large store, and whatever people ask for he should not have, and what he does have should not be requested.

A metzee fun a ganef
Literally, a bargain from a thief, refers to a good deal, a steal

By the time I used all the discount coupons, that dress cost so little it was *a metzee fun a ganef*.

Arumgeflikt
Literally, plucked on all sides; figuratively, robbed, swindled.

You paid too much for that property. You were *arumgeflikt*.

Balabost
Literally, "master of the house," used to refer to a boss, the owner of the business. The feminine, *balaboste*, can be the woman who's in charge, but is used more commonly to refer to a housewife, literally, "mistress of the house."

My great grandfather worked his way up from a piece worker in a sweat shop to the *balabost* of his own factory.

Women in the fifties would go to college, get married, and stay at home, but they discovered that being a *balaboste* did not earn them a lot of respect.

Bilik
Inexpensive.

I don't want to spend a lot of money for a DVD player. I saw one that was *bilik*, but I wonder if it is any good.

Draikop
Literally, one who turns another's head; a finagler; can also refer to the person who is befuddled.

I went to the appliance store thinking I knew which dishwasher I wanted, and the *draikop* convinced me it was a waste of money and I needed to buy the more expensive model.

By the time he finished with his sales *spiel*, I was such a *draikop* I had no idea what I was signing.

Er zol altsting zen, un nit hobn mit vos tsu koyfn.
He should see everything, but have nothing to buy it with.

Ganef
A thief.

My landlord is such a *ganef*. He refused to return our security deposit, even though we cleaned up the apartment.

Ganaivishe shtiklekh
Literally, a piece of thievery; refers to sneaky actions.

Be careful doing business with him and his *ganaivishe shtiklekh*.

Gazlen

Robber, swindler.

That *gazlen* tried to charge me double.

Geherik; gehern

Appropriate, to belong.

Dos gehert nit tsu dir.

Literally, *that does not belong to you;* figuratively, *that's not your job. It is not your responsibility.*

Gelt

Money.

He doesn't care about whether he likes a job. All he cares about is how much *gelt* he can make.

Oif drei zakhen shtait di velt: oif gelt, oif gelt, oif gelt.

The world stands on three things: money, money, money.

Tsen shifn mit gold zol er fahrmorgn, un dos gantse gelt zol er fahrkrenkn.

Ten ships of gold should be his and the money should only make him sick.

Aroysgevorfene gelt

Wasted money, throwing good money after bad.

Buying that stock is *aroysgevorfene gelt*.

Hondel

To haggle, make a deal.

"To Jew someone down" is an anti-Semitic canard for hondling.

Kadokhes

Literally, chills and a fever; figuratively, worthless.

He thought he'd found a rare stamp, but it was *kadokhes*.

Kapsen

Cheapskate

He is such a *kapsen*, he will not put air conditioning in his factory.

Macher

Literally, a maker; refers to a big shot, a major player. The word is usually seen in English spelled with *ch*, but it is pronounced with the gutteral *kh*.

He thinks he's such a big *macher*, but he's just an assistant.

Maven

An expert. It can also be used sarcastically.

I can barely turn on the computer, but my ten-year-old grandson-the-genius is a real *maven*.

Zingn ken ikh nit, ober a maivin bin ikh.
I can't sing, but I'm an expert. (Those who can, do; those who can't, criticize.)

Metzee'ah

A find, a bargain.

They bought the house at a great price because the owners needed some quick cash. It was quite a m*etzee'ah*.

Mezuma

Cash.

I can give you a discount for *mezuma*.

Onsaltn

Literally, to add salt; figuratively, to sweet-talk.

Maybe if I try to *onsaltn* her, she'll give me a better deal.

Opgeflikt

Suckered.

I was *opgeflikt* into buying flood insurance when I didn't need it.

Opgekrokhshene skhoyre

Shoddy merchandise.

I won't shop there. Their *opgekrokhshene skhoyre* is not worth the money.

Oys shidukh

Literally, *the engagement is over*, figuratively, *the deal is off!*

When they offered me the job, they said it came with good benefits, but after I accepted their offer, they tried to cut them, so I told them, "*Oys shidukh.*"

Pushka

A box or canister for collecting *tzedaka* (charity)

Every convenience store has a *pushka* for all kinds of charities.

After the Jewish National Fund was established in 1901, its collection boxes became ubiquitous in Jewish homes and businesses. Its original goal was to purchase land from the Ottoman Empire that controlled Palestine. It also helped fund the first modern Jewish city Tel Aviv, financed the research and development projects of Jewish scientists, and aided the first kibbutzim. Its major

undertaking, one that continues today and is the reason the JNF is well-known to all Jewish school children even now, is reforestation—the planting of trees in Israel. Many a Bar *and* Bas Mitzvah *have trees planted in Israel in their honor.*

Shnorrer

A beggar, a panhandler, someone looking to get something for nothing. Can also be a professional fundraiser.

That *shnorrer* is always asking me to drive him to work, but he never offers to chip in for gas.

Don't bother returning her call. She is just *shnorring* for some charity or other.

In the 1930 movie Animal Crackers, *Groucho Marx rhymed "shnorrer" with "explorer" during the song "Hooray for Captain Spaulding." The song later became the theme for his TV game show* You Bet Your Life.

Shvindl

Sounds like its definition: to swindle, deceive.

He tried to *shvindl* the wrong person, and went to jail.

61

CHAPTER EIGHT

Ess, Ess, Mein Kind

Gastronomical Judaism

Nothing—celebrations, holidays, even *shiva* and fast days—takes place in Judaism without food. Many foods that are considered Jewish—for example, kreplach, blintzes, borscht—are common to many Eastern European countries.

Every Jewish holiday has its own traditional foods associated with it: *Challah, gefilte* fish, chicken, and *cholent,* a dense stew made of beans, potatoes, other root vegetables, and meat and slow cooked on a low heat, for *Shabbos* (Sabbath); a round *challah* and honey for *Rosh Hashanah* (New Year); any food with a mixture of ingredients, such as stuffed cabbage, to symbolize abundance, and pomegranates for *Sukkos* (Festival of Booths); anything fried in oil, such as potato *latkes* (pancakes) or Israeli *sufganiot* (donuts) for Chanukah; *hamantashen,* a triangular pastry filled with pureed fruit such as cherries, blueberries, apricots, prunes or *lekhvar* (poppy seeds), a symbol of Haman's three-cornered hat, for Purim; nuts and dried fruits—in other words, trail mix—or *bakhser,* carob, also known as Locust bean or St. John's bread (but not among Jews) for *Tu B'Shevas* (the fifteenth of the month of *Shevas,* the Jewish

Arbor Day); *matzo* (unleavened bread) and foods made with it for *Pesakh* (Passover).

Jewish foods have become popular and even mainstream in the U.S. "*Kosher*-style" or "Jewish" delis, serving so-called "Jewish" foods that are not necessarily *kosher* (pastrami with cheese, for example) can be found almost everywhere, not just in large cities. Bagels and lox are on menus in diners in rural areas as well as in metropolitan ones. In fact, bagels have become as ubiquitous as English muffins. And many Yiddish words for foods are familiar to English-speakers.

Babke

Coffee cake. Not to be confused with *bubkes*.

The *shul* keeps serving the same *babke* every week until it's gone. It's so freezer burned and stale no one will eat it.

Bialy

Similar to a *bagel*, but minus the hole.

My brother prefers a *bialy* to a *bagel*. He's such a slob that every time he eats a *bagel*, the cream cheese oozes out of the hole onto his shirt. There's no hole in a *bialy*, so his shirt stays clean, until he spills coffee on it.

The word bagel *comes from the Middle High German word* broug, *a ring or bracelet. It likely originated in the Polish town of Krakow. The word* bialy, *which is short for* bialystoker kuchen *(Bialystok's Cake), comes from the name of the Polish town of Bialystok.*

Blintz

An Eastern European version of a crepe, usually filled with farmer's cheese, blueberries, cherries, or apples, and served with either sour cream or apple sauce.

She's such a snob that she claims her *blintzes* are crepes.

Borscht

A soup made with beets and served hot or cold with a dollop of sour cream. It was a popular enough dish to have given its name to the Borscht Belt, the Jewish resort section of the Catskills where many comedians got their start, often as waiters. Not to be confused with *shav* (made with sorrel) or gazpacho (different ethnicity).

Hey, *klutz!* Careful you don't spill the *borscht*. You'll never get the stains out.

Bronfn

Whiskey.

Odem yesode meofe vesofe leofe—beyno-lveyno iz gut a trink bronfn.
A man comes from the dust and in the dust he will end—in the meantime, it is good to drink whiskey.

In a wonderful example of names being based on occupations, the Bronfman family of Canada, leading Jewish philanthropists, made its fortune through the liquor distillery Seagram's, of which Edgar Bronfman, Jr., is CEO.

Challah

The egg bread, often braided, used to celebrate the Sabbath.

They almost got a divorce over their argument about whether *challah* should be sliced thin or thick for French toast.

Ess nisht di challah fahr a moytse

Don't eat the challah *before you have made the blessing. In other words, don't have sex before marriage. (In English, we say, "Why buy the cow when the milk is for free?")*

Ess

Eat. Usually used as an exhortation as in the oft heard "*Ess, ess, mein kind*" (Eat, eat, my child.) There's an old pun about a Jewish cruise ship, the *Ess, Ess, Mein Kind.*

You're too skinny. *Ess.*

Farfel

Broken up pieces of *matzo.*

He's so dumb he thought I was talking about Shari Lewis's puppet when I said I needed to pick up some *farfel.*

Flanken

A cut of meat from short ribs, usually boiled or stewed.

In my opinion, *flanken* is one of the reasons many people think "Jewish haute cuisine" is an oxymoron.

Fleegl

Wing.

My grandmother always put the *fleegl* in the chicken soup pot. Buffalo wings were unknown in the *shtetl*!

Forshpeis
An appetizer.

When they come to our house for dinner, we serve a full-course meal, but when they invite us for dinner, all they serve is a *forshpeis*.

Fress
Not just to eat, but to be a glutton.

You better get to the buffet table before my cousin does. He's such a *fresser*, there won't be anything left for the rest of us.

Er frest vi a ferd.
He eats like a horse.

Gedempte fleish
Pot roast, brisket.

I don't like *gedempte fleish*. It's always over done.

Gefilt croyt; holeptses; holishkes; prokas
Stuffed cabbage; the names change depending on the country of origin.

My assimilated grandmother did not make *holishkes* or *prokas*. She made stuffed cabbage.

Gefilte fish
Literally, stuffed fish. When made from scratch, similar to meat balls, but with ground up carp, pike, or other white fish mixed with eggs (as a binder) and matzo meal or flour. Usually served these days from a jar. Always served with horseradish.

My *goyishe* neighbor loved the appetizer I served until she found out it was *gefilte* fish. She barely made it to the bathroom before she threw up.

Geshmakt
Delicious, tasty.

He told me gorgonzola cheese is quite *geshmakt*, but I can't stand the smell.

Gogl-mogl
A drink made from honey, warm milk, raw egg, and brandy or other hard liquor.

Whenever I had a sore throat, my grandmother would make me a *gogl-mogl*. It always made me feel sicker.

Gribenes
Crispy chicken skin; cracklings, usually fried with *shmaltz* and onions.

My cardiologist would have a fit if she knew I still eat *gribenes*.

Kasha
Buckwheat groats, a whole grain that is healthful if not made in the traditional way with shmaltz.

He gave me one of those pillows stuffed with buckwheat. It's so uncomfortable I wanted to open it up and cook the contents with *varnishkes* (bowtie pasta).

Khalushes
Disgusting, nauseating

I'm glad squid isn't *kosher*. I think it sounds *khalushes*.

Khrain
Horseradish.

He made his own *khrain* only once, but the *shlimazel* forgot to open a window and almost wound up in the hospital.

Kikhel

A crispy, concave, puffy, cookie coated with sugar.

It sounds like a weird combination, but chopped herring is great on *kikhel*.

Kishke

Stuffed derma.

I served him *kishke* but didn't tell him what it was until after he'd finished it and asked for more. He still hasn't forgiven me.

Kishke *is made from intestine casings filled with meat, flour, breading, and spices. It's not as disgusting as it sounds, and, unlike haggis, is baked not boiled.*

Knaidlakh

Matzo balls.

The first time she made *knaidlakh*, they came out like canon balls. Her mother-in-law has never let her forget it.

Knobl

Garlic.

It's traditional to eat *knobl* on Friday nights, because it's supposed to be an aphrodisiac.

Kremzel

Fried potato pancake. A *kremzel* is similar to a *latke*, but because it is made without flour, it is served for Passover, not Chanukah.

We tried to explain to the kids that chocolate chips and whipped cream didn't go well on top of *kremzel*.

Kreplakh

A filled flat dumpling made of noodle dough, a Jewish version of wontons or ravioli, and often served in soup.

Vilst esn bei meer kreplakh?

Do you want to eat kreplakh *with me? Said ironically, similar to the English, "Are you looking for a knuckle sandwich?"*

Kugel

A baked pudding, made with noodles or *matzo*, mixed with eggs and either onions and/or other chopped vegetables, or with cheese, apples, raisins, and/or other fruit.

Az me est Shabbes kugel, iz men di gantzeh vokh zat.

Eat kugel *on the Sabbath and be full all week.*

Galitzianers (Jews from Ukraine and Poland) prefer their kugel *sweet, while Litvaks (Jews from Lithuania and environs) prefer it savory.*

Latke

A potato pancake. Served with sour cream or applesauce.

She's such a phony. She served frozen *latkes* and tried to pass them off as homemade.

Lekekh

Honey or sponge cake.

She's the only one I know whose *lekekh* is either flat or not sweet enough.

Lokhshin

Noodles.

He's got *lokhshin* for brains.

69

Lox

Smoked salmon; Jewish sushi. Usually served on top of *bagels* with cream cheese.

You can dress it up all you want with capers and fancy crackers, but it's still *lox*.

The etymology of the word goes all the way back to the Proto-Indo-European word for fish, and cognates (lax, lakhs) can be found in many Teutonic and Scandinavian languages.

Mamaliga

Corn meal porridge; the Eastern European version of *polenta*.

I don't care how good it's supposed to taste, to me *mamaliga* is not *geshmakt*.

Mandelbrot; kamishbrot

Literally, almond bread; similar to twice-baked *biscotti*. *Kamishbrot* is the Ukrainian version of the same cookie.

I can't believe you'd spend $3.00 at a fancy coffee place for the same *mandelbrot* my grandmother used to make.

Matzo

The unleavened bread eaten at Passover.

I've found an inexpensive cure for diarrhea: eat enough *matzo* and you won't shit for a month.

Meichel

A treat.

When some women want a *meichel*, they buy shoes. I treat myself to an ice cream sundae.

Nosh

To snack, nibble between meals.

She can't figure out why she can't lose weight, but all she does is *nosh* on junk food all day.

Nosherei *is what you snack on, and often means junk food.* Nosherei *is similar to* khazerei, *which comes from the Hebrew word for pig, and always means junk food. A* nosher *and a* khazer *are slightly different, too. A* nosher *is someone who eats between meals, who "grazes," but a* khazer *stuffs his mouth full of food while noshing.*

Nusl

Nuts.

He always brings *nusl* to our house when we invite him for dinner. He hasn't noticed yet that we never serve them.

Peklflaish

Corned beef.

Hot *peklflaish* on rye bread with mustard is a real *meichel*. But serving it on white bread with mayo is a *shande*.

Petcha

Jellied calves feet.

He almost threw up when they served him *petcha,* a delicacy.

71

Shmaltz

Fat, particularly chicken fat; as an adjective, the word *shmaltzy* refers to anything overly sentimental.

I can't stand those *shmaltzy* shows on TV at Christmas time.

Shmaltz *was used to fry almost anything that could be fried. It has gone the way of other delicacies like gribenes (crispy chicken skin) and liver and onions. The advent of Crisco shortening was a major cause of rejoicing in many a kosher kitchen, since shmaltz was by its nature flaishik (meat) and could not be used in the preparation of dairy meals. Crisco, being made from vegetables, was parve (neutral) and could be used to fry any foods, and was used for baking parve pastries.*

Shmear

Sounds like "smear," which is what it is. It's what you put on your *bagel* when you want only a bit of cream cheese.

I'll take a poppy seed and a *shmear*.
Can also be used to refer to a bribe.

I'll *shmear* the ticket seller and get us better seats.

Shnaps

Generic term for liquor.

Who said Jews don't drink hard liquor? After services every day, the men used to get together for a *shtikl* herring and some *shnaps*.

Shpritz
Literally, spray. Usually refers to seltzer. When served by itself (instead of as a mixer), it's called "two cents plain."

Don't get too close to him; when he talks, he *shpritzes*.

Shmekn
To smell.

There's nothing like the *shmek* of frying onions and garlic.

A *fremdeh bissen shmekt zis*.
Another's tidbit smells sweet.

Smeteneh
Sour cream.

She was so *fahrshimlt* she used *smeteneh* instead of whipped cream on top of the ice cream sundaes.

Taam.
Taste, from the Hebrew word for taste, *ta'am*.

This brand of soup has no *taam*. It needs some *knobl*.

Batampt
Tasty. There is a brand of *kosher* condiments (pickles, sauerkraut) called BaTempte.

She thinks her turkey is *batampt*, but it's always too dry.

Oystaam
No taste; can refer either to flavor or to a sense of style.

She thinks she's such a good cook, but her food is *oystaam*.

There was a time when wearing white shoes after Labor Day was *oystaam*.

Umbatampt
Tasteless.

No one has the heart to tell him that his hamburgers are
umbatampt.

Taiglakh
Small pieces of dough covered in honey.

I tried to make *taiglakh* like my grandmother did at Rosh
Hashanah, so we'd have a sweet year. But mine are more
like a disastrous year.

Tzimmes
A casserole usually made with carrots and prunes, but also can
be made with sweet potatoes or other vegetables or fruits.
It refers also to overreacting to a troublesome or messy situation.

It's no big deal. I don't know why you have to make such a
***tzimmes* out of it.**

Zoyere ugerke
Literally, sour cucumber; pickle. (The word gherkin is from the
Slavic word for cucumber.)

You can't get a *zoyere ugerke* that's *batampt* from a jar. You
have to buy it from a barrel.

Zup
Soup.

Chicken *zup* might not cure the common cold, but it makes
it more bearable.

Von zup zu nislekh.
From soup to nuts.

CHAPTER NINE

Frailikh Zol Zein

It's a Good Life

Times may have been difficult for Jews in Eastern Europe, but they still knew how to celebrate a *simkha* (a happy event). And anything could qualify as a *simkha*, especially life cycle events.

There are rituals for every stage of a person's life, each event followed by a *seudas mitzvah*, a festive meal to mark the obligation. A baby is welcomed into the world by remembering the covenant God made with the Israelites through the *bris milah* (circumcision) for a boy and a naming ceremony for a girl. When children begin to learn to read, they are given wooden cutouts of the *alefbais* (alphabet) coated with honey, so they'll associate education with sweetness. The coming of age is marked by the *Bar* or *Bas Mitzvah* ceremony—and party. Weddings are so joyous they are traditionally divided into three parts: the engagement, the signing of the *kesubah* (contract), and the formal ceremony in front of witnesses and under the *khuppah*. (Today, most couples combine the three ritual elements into one ceremony.) Weddings are considered so important that they are held (although without the music and dancing) even if the family is still in mourning. And even death is marked by traditional foods: eggs to symbolize the cycle of life and renewal, pastries and candies to sweeten the mourners' lives.

Joyousness and celebration also marked holidays: *Shabbos* isn't complete without singing and dancing (albeit *a capella*, as it's forbidden to use musical instruments on the Sabbath). Purim is so much fun that the entire month is dedicated to frivolity: "Be happy, it's *Adar*" is the preferred greeting during the month. We are commanded on Purim to become so drunk that we no longer know the difference between "Blessed be Mordecai" (along with Esther, the hero of the story) and "Cursed be Haman" (the villain who wanted to kill all the Jews). It's also the only time that the Biblical prohibition against cross-dressing is lifted, with costumes an integral part of the celebration.

So be *frailikh* and use some of the following words.

Borekh Hashem
Thank God.

Borekh Hashem, it could have been worse.

Bis hundert un tsvantsik yor.
Until a hundred and twenty years. Moses lived to the age of one hundred and twenty, so the expression is a traditional blessing on birthdays and anniversaries.

If I can't eat *shmaltz*, I don't want to live *bis hundert un tsvantsik yor*.

Glick
Luck.

Just my *glick*—I found the perfect dress for the wedding in the first store I went to, and then found out my sister was wearing the same one.

Himmel
Heaven, sky.

Gott im Himmel, did you see that guy run the red light?

Laiben ahf dein kop!
Life on your head; Good job! Nice work! (Can be sardonic.)

You mixed up the *milchik* and *flaishik* utensils. *Laiben ahf dein kop!*

Mekhei'ya
A reviver; a relief.

I love my sister, but she can talk on and on about nothing. It's a real *mekhei'ya* when she finally shuts up.

Nakhas; Shep nakhas
Pride; to take pride in.

They're the kind of grandparents who *shep nakhas* if their grandchildren don't flunk any courses.

Nisht gerferalakh
No big deal.

Don't worry about spilling the soup. It was an accident. *Nisht gerferalakh*.

Oht azoy
Thusly.

I showed you a dozen times how to do it—*oht azoy*, just like that.

Olam Ha'ba

The world to come; can be the afterlife or the Messianic age.

My elderly neighbor plans to see her late husband again in *Olam Ha'ba*.

Nations will finally learn to get along—in *Olam Ha'ba*.

The question of whether Jews believe in Heaven and Hell can best be summed up by two words: "It depends." (Another oft heard two-word answer is: "Who knows?") Jews have an ambivalent and rather undefined view of the afterlife. Resurrection is a central tenet of traditional belief, occurring when the Messiah comes, which is one of the reasons Jews do not cremate bodies. The Talmud refers to the gilgul neshomos, *the revolution of souls, which the* Zohar, *the central text of Kabala and Jewish mysticism, interprets as reincarnation. Generally, however, the Jewish texts do not have much to say about an afterlife. For this reason, Judaism is considered an "earth-bound" religion, one that focuses more on our actions here rather than worrying about what will happen after.*

Pahst

Appropriate.

It was a difficult situation to be in, but his behavior was *pahst*.

Oib der shukh pahst, kenst im trogen.
If the shoe fits, wear it.

Shekhekheyanu

Literally, "Who has kept us alive," it is the first word of a prayer of thanks recited whenever there is a happy or special occasion or at the beginning of a new endeavor. The prayer blesses God "who has kept us alive, sustained us, and brought us to this time."

After three tries, he finally got his driver's license. He should say a *Shekhekheyanu*.

Yasher koyekh.

Congratulations, good job. (Can be ironic.)

After spending hundreds of dollars on lottery tickets, you finally won a few bucks? *Yasher koyekh*!

Compliments and Terms of Endearment

Saikhel

Common sense, brains, smarts. (Can be a compliment or a term of derision when used sarcastically.)

She realized she was being followed on a deserted road, and there was no cell phone reception, so she used her *saikhel*, drove to the closest convenience store, and leaned on her horn.

You can't wear sandals in the winter! Use some *saikhel*!

Ain mol a saikhel, dos tzvaiteh mol khain, dem dritten mol gil men in di tzain.
The first time it's smart, the second time it's cute, the third time you get a sock in the teeth.

A kindershe saikhel iz oikhet a saikhel.
A child's wisdom is also wisdom.

Shtarker

Someone who is strong, physically or emotionally. Can also refer to a bodyguard, bouncer, enforcer.

Don't try to be a *shtarker* and move that piano yourself. Get some help.

After his wife died, he had to be a *shtarker* for the children.

Tzaddik

A righteous person.

If we had saints in Judaism, that *tzaddik* would be one.

A tzaddik vos vais er iz a tzaddik iz kain tzaddik nit.
A righteous man who knows he is righteous is not.

Tzutzik

An ambitious or energetic person.

I get tired just thinking about everything that *tzutzik* does all the time.

Zeeskeit

Sweetie.

Can I get you anything else, *zeeskeit?*

Celebrations

Badkhen

Entertainer; jester.

In the movie *The Wedding Singer,* Adam Sandler's character was a *badkhen*.

A badkhen makht alemen frailikh un alain ligt er in dred.
A jester makes everyone laugh and he alone is miserable.

Bar Mitzvah

The coming-of-age ritual for a boy.

His *Bar Mitzvah* reception was more about the bar (as in free drinks) than the *mitzvah* (good deeds).

The two-word phrase Bar Mitzvah *literally means "son of the obligation," and indicates a boy who is thirteen and has attained the legal status of an adult. The responsibility for keeping Jewish traditions and rituals now passes from his parents to him. The phrase has come to refer to the service at which the boy is first counted in the* minyan *(quorum of ten adults for a public prayer service). At that time, he is called to the* bimah *(literally, stage) to do the blessings before the reading of the* Torah *scroll. These days it also means the party marking the occasion. Once a boy turns thirteen, however, he is a* Bar Mitzvah *and has the legal status of an adult even without the ritual or the party.*

Bas Mitzvah

The coming-of-age ritual for a girl.

I've been to weddings less lavish than her *Bas Mitzvah* party.

The word bas *is the Ashkenazi pronunciation of the Hebrew word* bat, *which means "daughter," and a Bas Mitzvah is a twelve-year-old girl who is now of legal age. (In addition to now being responsible for keeping the* mitzvos, *she was also considered old enough to marry under Jewish law.) There was no formal ceremony to*

mark the occasion until March 18, 1922, when Rabbi Mordecai M. Kaplan, the founder of Reconstructionist Judaism, developed a synagogue ritual for his oldest daughter, Judith. In these days of equal rights, rites, and responsibilities for girls and women, the Bas Mitzvah *ceremony is indistinguishable from the* Bar Mitzvah *one, and is also held at the age of thirteen. In more traditional synagogues, the age is still twelve and the girl is called to the* bimah *on Friday night, when the* Torah *scroll is not removed from the* aron kodesh, *the holy ark.*

Draidel

A spinning top, used in a gambling game at *Chanukah*.

He is so hyper—he looks like a *draidel* that keeps spinning.

The word draidel *comes from* drai, *the Yiddish word for turn. The game is played for* gelt *(money), either real coins or chocolate ones, called* Chanukah gelt.* *Each side is labeled with a Hebrew letter:* Nun, *for* nes *(miracle);* gimmel, *for* gadol *(great);* hai, *for* haya *(was);* shin, *for* sham *(there). The resultant sentence means, "A great miracle happened there," referring to the apocryphal story of the one-day's supply of consecrated oil for the Temple that lasted the eight days. (In Israel, the final letter is* pai *for the word* po, *"here," so the sentence is, "A great miracle happened here.") Depending on which letter is showing when the top stops spinning, the player gets nothing (*nun*), half (*hai*), all (*gimmel*), or has to add to the pot (*shin*).*

---

*Shameless self promotion: Check out the cozy mystery *Chanukah Guilt* (no it's not a typo; it's a pun), written by this author.

Fahrbrengen
A party or gathering, especially religious or family

We went to a *fahrbrengen* last weekend. There was just as much dancing as there was study.

Fahrpitzed
Dressed up.

Aren't you a bit *fahrpitzed* to go to a movie?

Fahrshnoshked
Drunk.

I could not believe how strong that Cosmopolitan was— after one, I was completely *fahrshnoshked*.

Fahrtootsed
Overdressed, overdone.

She always comes to work all *fahrtootsed*, but most of us just wear jeans.

Kapelye
Musical band.

I hate going to a party that has a DJ. The DJ's are always so *shmultzy*. So we decided to have a *kapelye* instead.

The iconic Jewish song Hava Nagillah *is Hebrew, not Yiddish. And it's not an ancient traditional song either. The tune is of Chasidic origin, but the lyrics, which are attributed to Abraham Zevi Idelsohn, may actually have been written by his student, Moshe Nathanson—who was twelve years old when his teacher gave him the task of coming up with lyrics to the wordless melody in 1907.*

Kumsitz

Literally, come sit; figuratively, a sing-a-long, often around a campfire.

The youth group tried to end every meeting with a *kumsitz*, but most of the kids would sneak off for a smoke.

Ongepatchket

Overdressed, overdone.

She looks so *ongepatchket* with all that makeup on.

I have never seen a house with so many *tchotchkes*. It's really *ongepatchket*.

Tummler

Entertainer, slapstick comic, from the Yiddish word for noise, *tummel*.

A lot of standup comics got their training as *tummlers* in the Borscht Belt.

He thinks he's funny, but he's just a *tummler*.

Weddings

A wedding is one of the most important and joyful rites in Judaism. One of the first blessings given to newborns, when they are formally given a name, is "May [he or she] grow into a life of *Torah, khuppah, oo'ma'asim tovim*—Torah (learning), the bridal canopy (marriage, or family devotion), and good deeds."

A khissoren, di kalleh iz tsu shain.

To a fault-finder, even the bride is too pretty.

Alte moyd
Old maid.

In some traditional communities, an unmarried girl of eighteen is already an *alte moyd*.

Alter bokher
Bachelor.

My uncle is an *alter bokher*. My mother thinks he's gay, but I think he's just afraid of commitment.

Aufruf
Literally, calling up. The *Torah* honor given to a groom (and nowadays to the bride, too) on the *Shabbos* before the wedding.

The *aufruf* was an embarrassment. The *khoson* didn't know the blessings.

Kallah
Bride.

She was the exception to the rule that every *kallah* is beautiful on her wedding day.

Kesuba
Marriage contract, from the Hebrew word for something written.

Instead of using a preprinted *kesuba*, they had one custom illustrated by a professional calligrapher. The problem is, he spelled the *kallah*'s name wrong.

Khasana
Wedding.

She started planning her daughter's *khasana* before she was born!

Khoson
Groom.

I have never see a *khoson* as nervous as he was.

Khuppah
Wedding canopy.

They decorated the *khuppah* with roses, and the maid of honor had an allergy attack on the *bima*.

Nokh di khuppah iz shpet di kharoteh.
After the khuppah, *it's too late for regrets.*

Makhatonim
The parents of one's daughter-in-law or son-in-law.

Their *makhatonim* didn't help out financially with the wedding, but insisted on criticizing everything.

Makhatonista
Mother-in-law.

My sister's *makhatonista* is the model for every mother-in-law joke.

Makhotin
Father-in-law.

He got along better with his *makhotin* than he did with his own father.

Shadkhan
Matchmaker.

A bokher a shadkhan, a moid a bubb—konnen nisht zein.
A bachelor a matchmaker, a spinster a grandmother—these cannot be.

A shadkhn must zein a ligner.
A matchmaker must be a liar.

Bei a shadkhn iz nito kain meese kallah.
According to a shadkhn, *there's no homely bride.*

Shidukh
Arranged marriage.

I threatened my daughter that if she doesn't meet someone soon, I'll find someone and make a *shidukh* between them.

Yikhes
Lineage, family connections; someone who has *yikhes* is a *yakhsn*.

He's a *nogoodnik,* but still managed to marry into a family with a lot of *yikhes*.

IMMIGRATION OFF
★ (3298)
24 MAY 20

CHAPTER TEN

Altsding Lozst Zikh Ois mit a Gevain
When Things Go Bad

Often, the difficulties and tragedies of Eastern European Jewish life far outweighed the joyous occasions. One of the most often heard expressions was "*Shver zu zein a Yid*—It's hard to be a Jew." Jews were often denied citizenship in the countries in which they lived, even if they had been there for centuries. Often forbidden to own land, Jews had a limited choice of occupations. Money lending was allowed, because it was considered usury and forbidden to Christians. (Yiddish was useful for commerce, because Jews from different countries in Europe were able to converse with each other.) It wasn't only the Jews' livelihoods but life itself that was precarious. They could not move freely from place to place or live anywhere they wanted. Expulsions were a fact of life, dating from Roman times to the Inquistion to Shakespeare's England, and continuing into the twentieth century. Persecution, blood libels, pogroms, and rapes were expected. (Although matrilineal descent, meaning that a child's status as a Jew is determined through the mother's rather than the father's religion, has its roots in Biblical times, many believe it is so the child conceived through the rape of a Jewish woman by a non-Jew during a pogrom would still be

Jewish.) And there are many Jewish fast days throughout the year that commemorate catastrophes that befell the Jewish people, from the destruction of both Temples in Jerusalem, the First by the Babylonians in 586 B.C.E. and the Second by the Romans in 70 C.E., to the more recent additions of Holocaust Memorial Day and Israel's Memorial Day for fallen soldiers. It is not surprising that there are so many Yiddish words for bad luck.

Misfortune

Af tzolokes
Bad luck.

He got brand new tires and, *af tzolokes*, drove over some broken glass in the middle of the street two days later.

Altsding lozst zikh ois mit a gevain

Everything ends in weeping.

Az okh un vai
Tough luck.

He just moved into a new house, and then got downsized. *Az okh un vai*.

Balagan
A noisy tumult, a mess.

I made the mistake of going to my *ainikl*'s third birthday party at an indoor amusement park. What a *balagan*! How can so few kids make so much noise?

The first time I tried to make hamantashen at home, the bag of flour broke all over the floor. What a *balagan*!

Fahrfallen

Doomed; predetermined bad luck.

It is *fahrfallen* that as soon as I put on a new pair of panty hose, I get a run in them.

Fintster un glitshik

Literally, dark and slippery; figuratively, miserable.

It's been a *fintster un glitshik* winter. I can't wait for spring.

Gehakhte tzores

Literally, chopped up; figuratively, terrible trouble.

I've had such *gehakhte tzores* lately. Nothing is going right.

Geshrei

Yell, shout.

He gave such a *geshrei* when he stubbed his toe, I thought he'd cut it off!

Nit gut

Not good.

Oy, the situation over in the Middle East is *nit gut. Nit gut.*

Shvakh

Weak.

He planned to sue his former boss for age discrimination, but then realized his case was *shvakh*—the guy they hired to replace him is the same age.

Tzoris/Af tzores

Trouble, in serious trouble.

I can't believe how much *tzoris* they're having selling their house. If they can't sell the house soon, they'll be *af tzores*.

Umglik

Misfortune, literally "unluck."

It was just their *umglik* to buy a house when it was a seller's market, and to have to sell it in a buyer's market.

Eyn umglik iz fahr im vainik.
One misfortune is too few for him.

Umglik binds tzunoif.
Misfortune binds together.

Vern a tel

To be ruined; a shamble.

I spilled grape juice all over my new sweater. *Vern a tel* if I don't soak it right away in cold water.

A tel *in Hebrew is the word for a hill or mound, and often it covers an archaeological site. Tel Aviv, for example, is Hebrew for Hill of Spring.*

Abuse—Physical And Psychological

Frosk

Slap.

When was the last time a girl gave a boy a *frosk* on the cheek for trying to kiss her?

Khoyzek; khoyzek makhn

Ridicule; make fun of.

We were just *khoyzek makh* about how he looks in shorts, but he got insulted. He can't take a joke.

Kitsel
Tickle.

Since when is a *kitsel* child abuse?

Klap
Hit.

He got me so mad I wanted to give him a *klap*.

A klap fahrgait, a vort bashtait.
A blow passes, a word lingers.

Mekheeleh
Forgiveness, pardon, but often used ironically or euphemistically.

Mekheela? **How dare you call me that!**

Vilst a kopeh in mehkeeleh arein?
Do you want a kick in the pardon-the-expression?

Potch
Tap, slap.

That *yenta* next door accused me of spanking my son. All I did was give him a *potch en tuches*.

In my day, if a boy tried to kiss a girl on the first date, he got a *potch en punim*.

Shmeis
Thrash; can be used metaphorically for a rousing defeat in a game.

All the sports *mavens* predicted the Red Sox would *shmeis* the Yankees, but the Yankees got a winning homer in extra innings.

Strashn
To threaten.

I know it's bad parenting to *strashn* and not follow through, but it's hard to break the pattern.

Tshepn
To pick on.

Don't *tshep* your little sister. You're being a bully.

Zets
Jab, poke; can be verbal as well as physical.

He gave me a *zets*, but I didn't think of a comeback until later that night. I wish I could think more quickly on my feet.

Confusion
Yiddish-speakers must have often been perplexed, as there are many synonyms for the condition.

Fahrblonget
Lost, confused

I am so *fahrblonget*, I have no idea if I added the sugar to the cake mix yet.

Fahrdrimmeled
Dreaming, daydreaming.

I must have been *fahrdrimmeled* while coming home from work tonight; I drove right past my street.

Fahrklempt

Unpleasantly surprised, distraught, choked up, extremely emotional.

When my neighbor discovered her winning lotto ticket was just a gag gift from her husband, she was quite *fahrklempt* and made him sleep on the couch that night.

Fahrklempt *comes from* klempn, *the Yiddish word for* "tug," *and was popularized by Mike Myers'* Saturday Night Live *character Linda Richman, a suburban Jewish matron talk show host. When using the word, Myers would fan his face and pat his chest, as though the character was having heart palpitations (or a hot flash).*

Fahrmished

Mixed up, messed up.

I am usually pretty good at figuring out how to use a database program, but this one has me *fahrmished*.

Fahrmutshet

Tired out.

I am so *fahrmutshet* I can't think straight.

Fahrpatshket

Messed up.

You'll have to explain what happened again. I'm really *fahrpatshket*.

Fahrtshadet
Distracted.

I was so *fahrtshadet* at the staff meeting today, I didn't absorb a thing my supervisor said.

How To Use "Oy"

The interjection *oy* is commonly used as a response to bad news. In combination with other words, it takes on various degrees of seriousness:

Oy
Oh.

Statement: I got a flat tire. Response: *Oy*.

Oy vai
Oh, no.

Statement: I had a fender-bender. Response: *Oy vai*.

Oy vai iz mir
Oh, woe is me.

Statement: I went through a red light and broad sided another car. Response: *Oy vai iz mir*.

Oy gevalt
Oh, help.

Statement: The car was stolen. Response: *Oy gevalt*.

Oy, Gottenyu
Oh, my God.

Statement: The car was totaled. Response: *Oy, Gottenu*.

Other Expressions of Woe

When things are so bad it's not enough to say *oy*, try some of these words:

Genug iz genug

Enough is enough; often said in frustration, mostly by parents of toddlers or teenagers.

It is just been one thing after another. *Genug iz genug* already.

I told you before to turn down that CD player! It is giving me a headache. *Genug iz genug*!

Gehenem

Hell. If many Jews find it comforting to believe in *Olam Ha'ba*, they prefer not to believe in *Gehenem*. The word is not used as a curse (*dred*—ground—serves that purpose), but as a place name.

I hate my job. It is like being in *Gehenem*.

Gornisht helfen

Nothing helps.

My friend finally convinced her husband to go on Viagra, but unfortunately *gornisht helfen*.

Hak mir nisht kain tshaynik

Do not knock on my teakettle; in other words, stop pestering me.

Dinner will be ready when it's ready. *Hak mir nisht kain tshaynik*.

Halevei

If only! It should only be!

Maybe these new talks between the Israelis and Palestinians will succeed, *halevei*.

Khas vesholem
God forbid.

He is going to the doctor today for a stress test. I hope there's nothing wrong with his heart, *khas vesholem*.

Nechtiker tog
Literally, a night-like day; figuratively, yesterday's news.

Stop *hakn mir nisht kain tshaynik* about losing your keys. Forget about it already! *Nechtiker tog*. It is done and over with.

Pahst nisht
Inappropriate.

They didn't invite their daughter's *makhatonim* to their anniversary party. *Pahst nisht*. It's just not the right way to act.

Shtinkt; Es shtinkt
Stinks.

The school board just cut the music program. *Es shtinkt*.

Shande
Shame, scandal, embarrassment, usually before the *goyim* (non-Jews) or the *kinder* (children); most commonly heard as in the following two examples:

Es iz a shande fahr di goyim.
It's a shame in front of the non-Jews that he was arrested at the synagogue.

Es iz a shande fahr di kinder.
She just found out he has been shtupping *his secretary and filed for divorce. It's a shame for the children.*

A fremder nar iz a gleckhter; an aigener—a shand.
A strange fool is a laughing stock; your own—an embarrassment.

Shande un a kharpe
A shame and a disgrace.

The conditions in that nursing home are a *shande un a kharpe*.

Shandhoiz
Literally, house of shame, a whorehouse.

I don't want my daughter to pledge that sorority. I heard it's nothing more than a *shandhoiz*.

Shund; Shund-roman
Trash; trashy novel.

I have to admit that reading a *shand-roman* is one of my guilty pleasures.

Superstitions

Jews, both Ashkenazim and Sephardim, have a lot of superstitions. Modern followers of Kabbalah did not invent the red thread, nor were trendy urban architects the first to paint front doors blue. Both are designed as protective amulets to ward off the evil eye. Not all superstitions are negative, though.

Bashert
Predestined, intended; can be used for an event or a person.

As soon as they met, he knew she was his *bashert*. He asked her to marry him on their third date, and they've just celebrated their 55th anniversary.

Az es bashert ainem dertrunken tzu verren vert her dertrunken in a leffel vasser.
If one is destined to drown, he will drown in a spoon of water.

Dybbuk

The soul or ghost of a deceased person who cannot find rest and inhabits the body of a living person.

That poor girl in *The Exorcist* was possessed by a *dybbuk*.

In 1914, the writer S. Ansky penned a play in Russian, later translated into Yiddish, called Der Dybbuk, oder Tzvishn Tvei Veltn *("The Dybbuk, or Between Two Worlds"). His story of a young bride possessed by the spirit of a suitor who had died of love when refused her hand in marriage was one of the most popular plays of the Yiddish theater. It premiered in Warsaw, as a tribute to Ansky, after his death in 1920. The next year, it was produced in New York by Maurice Schwartz of the Yiddish Art Theater. Shortly thereafter, it was translated into Hebrew by Hayim Nachman Bialik, Israel's premier poet, and performed in Moscow by Habima the National Theater of Israel, which continues to present* The Dybbuk. *The play was also made into a Yiddish-language film in Poland in 1937, and a ballet by Leonard Bernstein.*

Gilgul

Reincarnation of a dead being, from the word for wheel.

She says her dog is the *gilgul* of her dead husband. He sleeps in the same bed with her, snores, steals the sheets, and pretends she's not there.

Golem

A creature formed from clay to protect the Jewish community of Prague; by analogy can refer to a person who's a dummy, doesn't think for himself.

Mary Shelley was familiar with the story of the *golem* when she wrote "Frankenstein."

In England, they'd describe that *golem* as "thick as two planks."

Although there are many earlier references to the Golem, the first printed version involving Rabbi Judah Loew of Prague appeared in Galleri der Sippurim (A Gallery of Stories) in 1847. Yudl Rosenberg's fictional account was published in 1909. According to the story, the emperor threatened the Jewish community of Prague with expulsion or death. Rabbi Loew formed a human figure from clay, placed the word emet (truth) on its forehead, and by reciting incantations, breathed life into it. At first, the Golem protected the community, but then became more and more violent. The emperor begged Rabbi Loew, who was becoming concerned the Golem would turn on its creator, to destroy it. In return, the Jewish community would be allowed to live in peace. Rabbi Loew destroyed the Golem by erasing the first letter of emet, transforming the word into met, death. According to legend, the lifeless Golem is hidden in the geniza, the attic, of the Alte-Neue Shul (Old-New Synagogue) in Prague.

Kenahora

The elision of the Hebrew phrase *k'neged ayin harah*, against the evil eye; usually preceded or followed by spitting three times over one's shoulder or through one's open fingers. Since spitting is frowned upon in polite society, and is illegal in many public places, the phrase *tu-tu-tu* is substituted.

The baby is beautiful, *kenahora*. *Tu-tu-tu*.

Shaidim

Demons.

Di gantzeh velt iz ful mit shaidim; treib zia khotsh fun zikh arois.
The whole world is full of demons; you just exorcise them out of yourself.

CHAPTER ELEVEN

Shlemiels, Shlimazels, and Shlubs
How to Insult Someone

From the number of insults in Yiddish, you could get the impression that Eastern European Jews didn't like their neighbors very much. Or the elderly. Or bratty kids. Or fools. Or the lazy. Or gossips. Or those lacking social graces. Or snobs. Or hypocrites. Or even family members (their own or their neighbors').

One characteristic of Jewish humor is that it is self-deprecating. We laugh at ourselves to deflect the cruelty of others' scorn and to undercut the sting of their negative stereotypes. In the same way, when we insult others, we feel better about ourselves. And when people live in circumstances in which they are considered sub-human, they need to use whatever tools they have to feel better about themselves. We insult others to undermine their ability to insult us.

Just as with curses, some of the most cutting insults are those that could be a compliment. Who would be insulted to be called a *melamed*, a teacher of young children? Someone with aspirations to be a college professor would be. After all, if he's such a scholar, why is he teaching children?

And other words are considered insulting by the recipient, even though the speaker may not have intended them to be. *Goy, shiksa, shaigitz,* and *shvartze* all fall within this category. Another word is *faigele,* which literally means a little bird and is used to refer to a gay man. An older generation may have been heard to say, "Such a good-looking boy, but he is 40 years old already and never been married. Do you think he is maybe a [whispered] *faigele*?" (Of course, these same people would be the ones who would condemn idle gossip.)

So when you want to insult someone without their knowing it, try some of these Yiddish words.

Alter tairekh
Old fool.

Imagine taking karate at his age—I wish he'd stop acting like an *alter tairekh*.

Alte makhsheife
Old witch.

The *alte makhsheife* down the street gets angry whenever a young kid rides a Big Wheels trike in front of her house.

Alter trombenik
Old blowhard.

That *alter trombenik* is always bragging about the great real estate deals he's made. So how come he's still living in the row house his parents bought in 1950?

Amorets
Literally, person of the land; boor, ignoramus.

He means well, but he's such an *amorets*. I'm surprised he can function in real life.

Arumshlepper

A rootless person.

I wish my grandson would find a good job already and stop being such an *arumshlepper*.

Azes ponim

Such a face; said sarcastically about someone who is impudent, a wise guy.

There's an *azes ponim* in my class who shows no respect at all for authority.

Balagole

Literally, a wagon driver; boorish, vulgar type

She's a lawyer. I don't understand what she sees in that *balagole*. I wouldn't be surprised if she's afraid of him.

Batlen

Idler.

I don't know how my nephew's managing to stay in college. That *batlen* would rather play video games than study.

Ben kalba

Son of a bitch.

I was waiting in line at the movie theater when a *ben kalba* snuck into line and got the last ticket!

Dumkop

A dummy, a dolt, someone stupid

What kind of *dumkop* would try to light a barbecue grill using kerosene?

Fahrbissene
Crabby.

I am sorry to be in a *fahrbissene* mood today, but I did not sleep well last night.

Fahrshimlt
Moldy.

I hate going swimming with him. I don't think he ever washes his towels; they smell *fahrshimlt*.

Fahrshlepte krenk
Literally, a long illness; figuratively, an obnoxious person

Have you ever met such a *fahrshlepte krenk*? I hate having to work with her on this project. She always acts as though everyone else is beneath her.

Fahrshlofener
Sluggard.

Stop being a *fahrshlofener* and take out the trash already. How many times do I have to ask?

Fahrshluggine
Beaten up, ratty.

This *fahrshluggine* car is always breaking down.

Mad Magazine's parody of the movie *Batman Forever* was called "Batman Fershlugginer."

Fahrshtunkene
Stinky.

You broke your promise to help me out first thing this morning. A broken alarm clock is a *fahrshtunkene* excuse.

Fahrshvist

Sweaty.

I hate hot flashes. I feel *fahrshvist* all the time.

Gridzhen

Literally, gnaw or chew noisily; figuratively, nag.

Stop *gridzhen*; I said I'll take out the trash, and I will. Later.

Hakhem

A wise man, a sage, (used sarcastically to refer to a know-it-all),

He thinks he such a *hakhem*, but he barely graduated from high school.

Khamoyer du ainer!

You ass!

Khamoyer du ainer! Look what you did to my car! Watch where you're going!

Khevraman

Happy-go-lucky, irresponsible.

Sure, he's fun to be around, but I wouldn't count on that *khevraman* to complete any important task.

Khnyok

Bigot.

Her father is such a *khnyok* that he refuses to accept his African-American son-in-law, even though he's Jewish.

Kibitz

Not to be confused with a kibbutz, an Israeli collective farm, kibitz is a nice way to say "gossip." Compare with *shmooze* and *yenta*.

My sister drives me up the wall; she always seems to
know when I'm busy and then calls just to *kibitz*. Then she
gets angry at me for wanting to hang up.

A *kibitzer* is someone who is a chatterbox, but is not quite so nosy
a busybody as a yenta.

I bumped into my neighbor in the supermarket and could
not get away from her. What a *kibitzer*.

Klafte
Bitch.

That *klafte* at work told my supervisor that I had gone to
lunch with my boyfriend instead of with a client.

Klainer gornisht
A little nothing.

He thinks he's so important, but he's just a *klainer gornisht*.

Knaker
Big shot, know-it-all, braggart.

I can't stand talking to that *knacker*. He's always bragging.

Kokhleffel
Cooking ladle; figuratively one who "stirs the pot" with rumors or
gossip.

If you want to know the dirt on anyone in the *shul*, just ask
that *kokhleffel*. Her information might not be accurate, but
it is juicy.

Kom vos er krikht
Literally, come whatever, he crawls; figuratively, a slowpoke.

It makes sense for me to carpool with my neighbor, but he
always makes me late for work. *Kom vos er krikht*. He'd be
late for his own funeral.

Kundis
Brat.

She thinks her son's a little angel, but he's a *kundis*.

Lekish
Dummy, fool.

Only a *lekish* would try to pay with an expired credit card.

Lemishke
Ineffectual.

He's too much of a *lemishke* to be a good schoolteacher.
The kids walk all over him.

Laidikgaier
Literally, an empty walker; figuratively, an idler.

No one wants to do a team project with him because he's
too much of a *laidikgaier*.

Mazik
Impish child.

Her son is such a *mazik*, but he's so cute it's hard to stay
angry at him.

Mamzer
Both literally and figuratively a bastard. In the legal sense, it refers
to a child conceived through an adulterous relationship. In the colloquial sense, it is used the same as in English.

Can you believe that *mamzer* broke up with her just before
her finals?

Az di muter shreit oifen kind, "Mamzer!" meg men ir gloiben.
When a mother yells at her child, "Bastard!" you can believe her.

Nar; narishkeit
Fool; foolishness.

Only a *nar* would give up a good paying job to go off to meditate at a commune in the middle of nowhere.

Stop this *narishkeit* now! You are not getting a tattoo, and that's the end of it!

Tattoos and body piercings are frowned upon in Judaism, tattoos because they are considered to be a form of self-mutilation and an imitation of idolaters, and piercings because they are faddish and may interfere with personal hygiene. Ear piercing is permitted for women, however, because it is considered ornamentation.

Nebbish
An ineffectual guy, a nobody; the Anglicized version of *nebekh*.

I don't understand what she sees in such a *nebbish*. Not only does he have the personality of a blank piece of paper, but he can't even hold down a job.

He's such a *nebbish* he just got fired as a shelf stocker at the convenience store.

Nishtikeit
A nothing.

He thinks he's a big shot, but he's just a *nishtikeit*.

Nokhshlepper
Literally, to drag along after; figuratively, a hanger-on.

109

My little brother is always tagging along with me. I wish he'd get his own friends and stop being a *nokhshlepper*.

Noodge

Similar to a nudnik, a *noodge* is a persistent pain in the neck. Sometimes seen spelled as *nudge*, but that spelling is too similar for the word that means to elbow someone or something out of the way. Most *noodges* can push you over the edge, though.

My son is being such a *noodge* about going to Disney World.

Ongebloozen

Sulking.

She's fifteen, so of course she's always *ongebloozen*.

Ongeshtopf

Literally, overstuffed; figuratively, loaded with money

They're complaining they have to get a new car, but they can afford one. They are *ongeshtopf*.

Opgelozen

Careless dresser.

I'm such an *opgelozen*—today I wore two different shoes.

Oysgemutshet

Tired out.

She's doing too much. She looks really *oysgemutshet*.

Oysshteler

Show off, braggart.

The *oysshteler* in the next office spent the whole day talking about his new boat.

Oyverobotl

Absent-minded.

They say that forgetting where you put your keys is just being normally *oyverobotl*.

Paskudne ; paskudnik; paskudnitse

Gross, nasty; a disgusting person.

How can anyone be friends with that *paskudne*? Belushi was funny when he started the food fight in *Animal House*, but it's not funny in real life.

Paskudnyak

Scoundrel.

She found out the guy she was dating was engaged to someone else. What a *paskudnyak*.

Pisher

Pishn means "to urinate," so a *pisher* is often used as an affection-ate term of derision for a barely toilet-trained toddler and, by exten-sion, for anyone who tries to do something beyond his ability.

That little *pisher* has been on the job for a week and already thinks he knows more than I do.

Potchke

Do too much, be obsessive.

The house looks fine. Don't *potchke* so much.

Prust

Rough, coarse; socially unrefined.

She may have grown up in a trailer park, but she's not *prust*. She has really made something of herself.

Prustak

A vulgar person.

He's a real *prustak*. He sees nothing wrong with swearing loudly in public.

Ruf mikh knaknisl

Literally, *call me a nutcracker*; figuratively, "sticks and stones."

Ruf mikh knaknisl, I don't care about your opinion of me.

Shikker

Drunkard.

It's okay to have a drink once and a while, but he's a *shikker*. I don't think I've ever seen him sober.

Shlekht vayb

Literally, a bad wife; figuratively, a shrew.

She better learn not to be a *shlekht vayb* or her husband will look elsewhere for some appreciation.

Shlemiel

A dorky guy.

He's such a shlemiel, I can't imagine fixing him up with any of my friends. They'd never speak to me again!

Shlimazel

A guy who never gets a break.

What a *shlimazel*! He quit his job when he thought he had a new one, and before he started working there, the company went bankrupt.

A shlimazel falt oifen ruken un tseklapt zich dem noz.
A shlimazel *falls on his back and hits his nose.*

The classic definition of the difference between a *shlemiel* and a *shlimazel*: A *shlemiel* spills his soup; the *shlimazel* is the one he spills it on.

Shlub

Sounds like slob, and that's what a *shlub* is. Usually someone slovenly, ill mannered, coarse, boorish. Sometimes transliterated as *zhlub*.

Homer Simpson is a loveable *shlub*.

Shlump, shlumper, shlumpy; shlumperdik

Disheveled, messy.

He is a big guy, but he doesn't look like a *shlump*. He is always well groomed.

My neighbor sits out on the front steps in a dirty T-shirt drinking beer from the bottle. He is a real *shlumper*.

We are going out to dinner with Bubbe and Zaide. Go put on a clean shirt. You look *shlumperdik*.

Shmendrick

Fool, nincompoop, a pipsqueak.

The early Woody Allen characters always acted like *shmendricks*.

Shtik holtz

Piece of wood; a person with no personality.

Whenever a blind date isn't too attractive, she's described as having a nice personality. Well, this one is both a *meeskeit* and a *shtik holtz*.

Shtipper

Brat.

I hate to say it about my sister, but her son is becoming a real *shtipper*. If he doesn't get what he wants, he has a temper tantrum until she gives in.

Shtunk

A stinker, a nasty person.

His father's a real *mensh*, but he's a *shtunk*. After his father retires, I'm finding a different insurance agent.

Shvuntz

A coward.

Don't be such a *shvuntz*. That dog's not going to bite you.

Trombenik

A phony, a braggart.

The *trombenik* down the street said he bought his wife a diamond tennis bracelet, but I saw him at the cubic zirconia counter at Wal-Mart the other day.

Tsatske

Bauble (like *tchatchka*); figuratively, a cheap woman.

Those skimpy clothes make her look like a *tsatske*.

Umgelumpert

Awkward, clumsy.

I feel sorry for my sixth-grade students. The girls are becoming young women and the boys are still in the *umgelumpert* stage.

Vilde chaya

Wild animal, a hyper child.

Their son's a *vilde chaya*, but their attitude is that boys will be boys.

Vilder mensh

A wild person.

He never settled down, but is a *vilder mensh*, drinking, gambling, getting into fights.

Vonts

Literally, a bedbug; figuratively, a mischievous child.

That *vonts* put salt into the sugar bowl.

One of the classic episodes of the television series M.A.S.H. had a subplot featuring a crossword puzzle none of them could complete. The clue that had them stumped: Yiddish for "bedbug." Of course, the word was vontz.

Yakhne

A coarse, loud-mouthed woman; a gossip; a busybody.

I bumped into that *yakhne* at the supermarket and I was so embarrassed by her braying laugh and insistence on telling me all about our neighbor's divorce.

Yenta

A busybody, a gossip.

I'd never tell her a secret. She is such a yenta.

Yetebedam

An intimidating man.

I usually speak my mind, but that *yetebedam* scares me.

115

Yold

A yokel.

I had to be nice to him because he's a customer, but when we went to lunch, the *yold* wiped his mouth on his sleeve.

Yungatch

A brat.

He is a *yungatch* now, but a little discipline could set him straight.

Yutz

A stupid person.

Don't be such a *yutz*. You understand exactly what I am saying.

CHAPTER TWELVE

Lokh in Kop

The Basics of Body Language

There are, of course, Yiddish words for all the parts of the human body, as well as ones that are specific to male and female anatomy. Not surprisingly, many of the male and female body part words are considered obscene or, at the very least, vulgar, including seemingly benign euphemisms. Those words that are not acceptable in mixed (or not) company are listed in the next chapter on the "Dirtiest Yiddish" words. The ones below may be coarse, but can be said, if not in mixed company, then during casual conversations with those of the same gender.

Others words for the human body are also used to refer to chicken parts and other foods: *pulkes, fis, gorgl*, even *tuches* (for the tail stump) are commonly heard. And some people love cow's *tsung*. The word *kishke* is interesting, as it changes meaning from a food item made with animal intestines to the actual intestines depending on whether the word is singular or plural.

Many of these body parts are the targets for Yiddish curses. How better to place a hex on enemies than by wishing them physical distress or harm? In the time before antibiotics and immunizations, any physical affliction could become fatal. A stomach cramp

117

might be the result of too much onions fried in *shmaltz,* or could be a perforated ulcer or appendicitis. A broken bone could lead to permanent disability. Without teeth, one would not be able to enjoy most foods. Those who cast curses having to do with the body knew just how serious their threats were.

Bainer
Bones.

A kholaire im zain bainer.
A cholera in his bones.

Shtainer af zayne bainer.
Stones on his bones.

Zol di markh oprinen fun dayne bainer.
Your bones should be drained of marrow.

Zolst tsebrekhn ale dayne bainer az oft mol vi di brekhts di aseres hadibres.
You should break your bones as often as you break the Ten Commandments.

Boykh
Belly, stomach.

A kapn im in zain boyakh!
A cramp in his stomach!

A makek im zayn boykh, a ruekh in zayn tatns tate arayn.
A plague in his belly, a devil in his father's father.

Az der mogen iz laidik iz her moi'ekh oilk laidik.
When the stomach is empty, so is the brain.

Es zol dir dunern in boykh, vestu maien az s'iz a homon klaper.
Your stomach will rumble so badly, you'll think it was Purim *noisemaker.*

Zi iz geven a kurveh in di mames boykh.
She was a whore in her mother's stomach.

Zol dik kapn baym boykh.
You should get a stomach cramp.

Fis
Feet.

Some cooks like to throw the chicken *fis* into the soup pot, but at least they remove them before serving the soup.

Zol er tsebrekhen a fis.
He should break a leg.

Gederem
Bowels.

A kapn in di gederem.
A cramp in his bowels.

Gorgl
Neck, throat.

She's had a face lift and uses Botox, but her scrawny *gorgl* gives away her age.

***Helzel* is like *kishke*, but the casing is made from the chicken's *gorgl* rather than the intestines.**

I think I am coming down with something. My *gorgl* hurts. Maybe I should gargle?

Kishkes
Stuffed derma.

In addition to the dish called stuffed derma in English, kishkes means intestines. Even though stuffed derma sounds more appealing than stuffed intestines, the words are synonyms. In fact, the etymology of derma is the Yiddish word derme, the plural of darm, another word for intestine.

He should get a *kapn im di kishkes*.
He should get a cramp in his guts.

Kop
Head.

Ale tsores vos ikh hob oyf mayn hartsn, zoln oysgain tsu zayn kop.
All problems I have in my heart should go to his head.

Drai mir nit kain kop.
Literally, do not twist my head; figuratively, stop pestering me.

Fahrdrai zikh dem kop.
Literally, turn your head; figuratively, drive yourself crazy.

Gai shlog dayn kop in vant.
Go bang your head on the wall.

Klap en kop.
Hit on the head, as in "If you don't behave, I'll give you a klap en kop."

Lokh in kop.
A hole in the head, as in the oft-heard Yiddishism "I need it like a lokh in kop."

Zol dir klapn in kop.
It should bang in your head; may it only happen to you like to me.

Zol er lebn bis hundert un tsvantsik yor—on a kop.
He should live to 120 years—without a head.

Lipelakh
Lips.

He has *dininke lipelakh*, and you can't trust anyone with thin lips.

Moyl
Mouth.

A kleine veibeleh ken oikh hoben a groisse moyl.
A small wife can also have a big mouth.

Fahrmakh dos moyl.
Shut your mouth.

Nem on a fuln moyl vaser!
Literally, fill up your mouth with water; figuratively, keep your mouth shut.

Oygn
Eyes.

Baide oygn dayne zoln faln fun dayn kop, khas vesholem.
Both your eyes should fall out of your head, God forbid.

Zalts im in di oygn, feffer im in di noz.
Throw salt in his eyes, pepper in his nose.

Pulkes

Legs, thighs, usually plump ones.

Fat pulkes are cute on a baby, but not on a grown woman wearing a bikini.

Don't go eating the chicken *pulkes*. I'm saving them for the kids. If they don't want them, I'll cut them up (the *pulkes*, not the kids!) and throw them into the chicken soup.

Tsainer

Teeth. There are two versions of the same curse:

Zolst fahrlirn ale tsainer akhuts ainem, un der zol dir vai ton.
You should lose all your teeth except one, and that one should ache!

Zolst fahrlirn ale dayne tsain akhuts ainer, un in dem zolst hobn a shreklikher tsainvaitik.
You should lose all your teeth but one, and you should have a terrible toothache in it.

Tsung

Tongue.

I never liked *tsung*. It looks too much like a cow's tongue, which is what it is.

A behaimeh hot a langen tsung un ken nicht redden; der metsh hot a kurtseh tsung un tor nisht reden.
An animal has a long tongue and can't speak; a man has a short tongue and shouldn't speak.

A hiltsener tsung zol er bakumn.
He should grow a wooden tongue.

Du host a langer tsung!

Literally, you have a long tongue; figuratively, you have a big mouth.

Got zol gebn, er zol hobn altsding vos zayn harts glist, nor er zol zayn gelaimt oyf ale ayvers un nit kenen rirn mit der tsung.

God should bestow him with everything his heart desires, but he should be a quadriplegic and not be able to use his tongue.

Hinten

Rear end, buttocks, ass; the word is synonymous with *tuches*, but *tuches* is used only to refer to the buttocks, while *hinten* can also be used as a direction, just as "rear" in English can refer to either the body part or the direction.

Move to the *hinten*.

Vifil yor er iz gegangn oyf di fis zol er gain af di hent un di iberike zol er zikh sharn oyf di hintn.

As many years as he has walked on his feet, he should walk on his hands, and for the rest of the time he should crawl along on his ass.

Zaftig

Pleasingly plump.

A *Yiddishe maidl* (Jewish maiden) should be *zaftig* and have some meat on her bones, not like those scarecrows you see on TV.

Pupik

Bellybutton, naval. Often pronounced "pipik."

Can you believe all these young girls walking around with their *pupiks* hanging out?

Zol vaks tsibeles fun dayn pupik.
Onions should grow from your bellybutton.

Shnoz
A nose, usually a long one. Sometimes called a *shnozzola*.

Jimmy Durante, or if you prefer your cultural references to be literary, Cyrano de Bergerac, had the epitome of the *shnoz*.

Tuches
Rear end, buttocks. Anglicized as *tush*.

Stop being such a pain in the *tuches*.

A tuches un a halb.
Literally, a rear end and a half; figuratively, a voluptuous woman.

I don't like skinny women. I prefer one with *a tuches un a halb*.

A favorite saying among Jewish wives is "Never let your husband see more than half a tuches*"; in other words, keep some mystery in your marriage. Or, to be more cynical, you don't have to tell him everything.*

Tuches ahfen tish!
Ass on the table! Put up or shut up! (In English, we'd say, "Shit or get off the pot.")

Zolst lebn vi a tsibele, mit dayn kop in drerd und dayn tuches in di luft.
You should live like an onion, with your head in the ground and your ass in the air.

Male Anatomy

Of course, there are words that are only for men.

Baitsim

Testicles, from the Hebrew for "eggs"; a synonym for *chutzpah*, in the same way that "balls" and "nerve" can be used interchangeably in English.

I could not believe the *baitsim* on that guy, talking back to the traffic cop like that.

Petseleh

Little penis, usually derogatory, but can be used affectionately to refer to a toddler. From the Yiddish word *pitsel* (wee, tiny).

Look at that *petseleh* trying to imitate his older brother. He is so cute.

Shvants

Penis.

I have never seen an uncircumcised *shvants*.

Female Anatomy

And there are words used only for women.

Bristen

Breasts.

It's a fallacy that all Jewish women have large *bristen*.

Just as there are a lot of euphemisms and synonyms for "penis," so are there many for "vagina." All the following are ways to refer to a woman's private parts.

Dorten

Down there.

She had to have surgery *dorten* for female problems.

Knipl

Literally, the corner of a handerkerchief; figuratively, a nest egg; euphemistically, a hymen.

Her new husband was inexperienced, so she was able to fool him into thinking she still had an intact *knipl*.

Oysoy hamokom

Literally, that place, a woman's privates.

I have got an itch *oysoy hamokom*. It must be a yeast infection.

CHAPTER THIRTEEN

Trikhen a Forts

The Dirtiest Yiddish

The words below are considered obscene, vulgar, and coarse. Other words in the book are too, but these are the ones most likely to get your mouth washed out with soap. It is doubtful your bubbe—or even your zaide—ever used them, and they may not have even known them. At the very least, they'd never have admitted to knowing them.

Several of these words, among them *drek, putz, shlong*—are used by English speakers who have an idea what they mean but don't realize they are considered obscene in Yiddish. There's a certain irony that English speakers use these words to avoid using what they consider the more taboo Anglo-Saxon ones.

Some of these words have to do with defecation, some with the euphemisms used for male and female genitalia, and the rest, of course, with sex and sexual intercourse.

The Yiddish word for sex is *geshlekht*. It is not etymologically related to *shlekht*, which means bad. In fact, in Judaism, sex is seen as a positive act, and it is even a mitzvah for a married couple to have sex on *Shabbos*. One of the promises a groom makes to his bride—a promise codified in the *kesubah* (marriage contract)—is

127

sexual gratification. It is even said that if a man wants to conceive a son, he should make sure his wife has an orgasm. (And it many not be just superstition: there is modern scientific evidence that the contractions of a woman's vaginal muscles during orgasm help move the sperm along to their targeted egg.)

So next time you want to be "naughty" but not use the English equivalent, try one of these words:

Defecation

Drek
Shit; human dung, feces, manure or excrement; inferior merchandise or work; insincere talk or excessive flattery.

Drek af dem teller.
Literally, *shit on a plate;* figuratively, *worthless.*

Drek mit leber.
Literally, *shit with liver;* figuratively, *worthless.*

Shtik drek.
Piece of shit; shit-head.

Forts
Literally, fart; figuratively a jerk.

He is such a *forts*. There is nothing about him I like.

Du zolst nor fahrtsn in dred.
*You should only fart in the ground (*in other words, *in your grave).*

Oder a klop oder a forts.
Literally, *either a wallop or a fart.* in other words, *either too much or not enough,* similar to "feast or famine" in English.

Trikhen a forts.
Dried old fart.

Kak
Crap.

Alter Kaker
Old fart, often abbreviated in English as A.K.

When we went back to the college for our 40th reunion, we realized we are now officially A.K.'s.

Fahrkakt
Shitty, crappy, fucked up; from *kak*.

If this *fahrkakte* photocopier doesn't stop jamming, I'll never get the reports done in time for the board meeting.

Kak im on!
Defecate on him! The hell with him!

Kak zich oys!
Go take a shit for yourself!

Khei kak
Nothing, worthless, unimportant; literally human dung.

Shmuck
An asshole, a fool; derisive term for a man; from an obscene slang word for penis.

That *shmuck* saw me waiting for that parking spot, but snuck in around me.

Tuches
Ass.

I worked my *tuches* off for that company and then they treated me like a *khei kak*.

Kush in tuches arein!

Kush mir in tuches!
Kiss my ass!

Shtup es in tuches.
Shove it up your ass.

Tuchesleker

Literally, ass-licker; figuratively, a brown-noser, apple-polisher, ass-kisser.

You don't think he got the promotion on merit, do you? He's nothing but a *tuchesleker*.

Mel Blanc, who provided the voices for almost all the Loony Toons characters, had a license plate with the letters KMIT. When the official from the California Department of Motor Vehicles questioned him as to its meaning, Blanc said it stood for an old Jewish expression, "Know Me in Truth." It actually stood for "Kush Mir in Tuches."

Euphemisms for Male Genitalia

Putz
Slang for penis, derogatory term for someone who's not very nice.

He took credit for his associate's work. What a *putz*.

Aus der putz shteyt, der seychel gait.
When the putz stands up, the reason departs.

Er muz zein a yamputz, veil af der yaboshe hob ikh nit gezen aza ainem.
He must be a sea prick, because I have never seen such a one on dry land.

Groisser putz
Big penis; big prick. Always said in a derogatory or sarcastic manner, never as a description of physical attributes.

My supervisor is a *groisser putz*—he refused to let his secretary leave when her son was sent home sick from school.

Putznasher
Cocksucker.

Get out of my way! *Putznasher!*

Shlong
Literally, a snake, serpent; figuratively, a penis.

Did you see the *shlong* on that horse!

Euphemisms for Female Genitalia

Knish
An Eastern European pastry dish, dough filled with meat, potatoes, cheese, or other foods. Also a euphemism for female genitalia.

Heh, I know what I'd like to stuff her *knish* with.

After my teenaged son found out the other meaning of *knish,* he couldn't hear the word without sniggering.

Pirge
A meat pie or dumpling, similar to the Polish *piroge* (or to a *knish*); similar to "pussy" in English.

Hey, *tsatske*, let me see your *pirge*.

Zakh; shpil zakh

Literally, thing, plaything; figuratively, an obscene euphemism for female privates.

Let's go out tonight and see if we can score a *shpil zakh*.

Sex

Ayngefedemt

Literally, to thread a needle; a euphemism for sexual intercourse.

Er hot kainmol nit ayngefedemt.
He has never been with a woman.

Baren

Fornicate, fuck with: figuratively, to bother, annoy.

***Baren* with Don Corleone, and you'll find a horse's head in your bed.**

Shtup

Push, shove. One of many euphemisms for sexual intercourse.

***Nu*, do you think you'll get to *shtup* her tonight?**

Dusik

Slightly fucked up.

I have to go see my boss. The vacation schedule came out and is *dusik*.

Sholem Aleichem wrote a short story in 1909 called "A Mentsh fun Buenos-Ayres" ("The Man from Buenos Aires"). It was about a Jewish salesman from Argentina

named Motek, who said of the goods he sold: "'I supply the world with merchandise, something that everybody knows and nobody speaks of,' Motek said obliquely. 'What do I deal in? Not in prayer books, my friend, not in prayer books.'" Of course, these illegal activities, and the existence of large Jewish crime syndicates, led to increased anti-Semitism and promoted the stereotypes of Jews as corrupters of morals and despoilers of young women. According to some sources, the Portuguese word for pimp, cafetão, comes from kaftan, the long black silk robe worn by some Orthodox Jews.

Hais, kalt
Hot, cold.

Ikh bin hais.
I am hot, I am horny.

Ikh bin kalt.
I am cold, I am frigid.

As in many languages, including Hebrew and German, to say the temperature is making you shiver or sweat, you use the equivalent of "It is hot to me," and "It is cold to me." Otherwise, you're talking about your libido.

Meise
Literally, a story or tale, a deed; figuratively, an obscene euphemism for intercourse, similar to the English phrase, "I did her."

So, how was your date last night? Did you do the *meise*?

Trenen

Literally, to rip, rend, open a seam; figuratively, to screw, engage in the act of intercourse.

I had an awful cold and just wanted to *gai shlufen*, but my boyfriend wanted to *trenen*. I gave him a choice—leave me alone or sleep on the couch.

Gai tren zkh.

Go fuck yourself.

Yentsen

To fornicate, to whore, to screw in the metaphorical sense.

My boss tried to *yentsen* me out of my bonus.

It is not generally known that Jews were involved in the thriving international "white slave trade." Young, naïve Eastern European Jewish women would be promised jobs, and then forced to work in brothels. Others would fall for the charms of a handsome young man who would marry them, and then give them a ticket to, for example, Buenos Aires, saying he would meet them there later. In Argentina, they would be met by the madam, who, claiming to be the young man's aunt, would take them home with her and gradually introduce them to the realities of their new lives: sell your body or starve. Shunned by the Argentinean Jewish community, these women could not be buried in the Jewish cemeteries, and established their own burial society, in 1916, called the Jewish Benevolent and Burial Association, popularly known as the Society of Truth. The last burial there was in 1970.

There are two words for prostitutes, both of which are used as descriptions of professionals and as insults.

Kurveh

Whore, prostitute.

My husband ran off with that *kurveh*. We'll see how long she stays with him after my lawyer finishes taking him for all he is worth.

Nafkeh

Prostitute.

What kind of role model for young teenaged girls is that actress? She looks like a *nafkeh*.

There are two other words for whorehouse beside *shandhoiz*.

Heizel

Whorehouse.

There are so many different men going in and out of that apartment that I wonder if it is a *heizel*.

Nafkeh baiis

Whorehouse.

Did you see the news? They raided that message therapy place down the street. It was a front for a *nafkeh baiis*.

Jewish prostitutes accounted for 17 percent of known prostitutes in Warsaw in 1872. In Krakow, the number was 27 percent, and in Vilna 47 percent. By 1889 Jewish women ran 70 percent of the licensed brothels in the Jewish Pale.

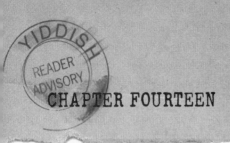

CHAPTER FOURTEEN

Oy, Ikh Darf Zikh Oyspishn—Geferlekh!

Other Useful Words

There are quite a few other Yiddish words that can be interspersed in conversation to make it more interesting. Some will be familiar to English speakers, while others will cause your listeners to mentally shrug and think 1) that you are a brilliant and erudite multilinguist; 2) that you are a pretentious poser (is there any other kind?); or 3) that you have no idea what you're talking about. I would not recommend using too many of these expressions with someone who may be familiar with Yiddish, as that person might strike up an entire conversation with you in that language. If that should happen, look thoughtful, nod, occasionally shrug and say, *"Nu,"* and try to escape before the Yiddish speaker realizes you haven't understood a word.

The words that follow are in common usage, and with the exception of the bodily functions, are everyday objects, events or places. Again, except for those words dealing with bodily functions, most of them are not vulgarisms, but part of daily life: clothing, school, synagogue, family relationships, religious rituals, expressions. Without knowing them, you will not understand the references many Jews make, whether in person or in the media.

No one needed to be taught how to keep a kosher home; it was ingrained from youth and done as a matter of course. Synagogue and home religious rituals were learned through example and practice, not by attendance at the occasional holiday service or going to religious school a couple of hours a week, if it didn't conflict with soccer.

Of course, these are generalizations. There were plenty of Yiddish speakers who were not religious, did not wear "Jewish" clothing, ate pork, worked on *Shabbos*. There were differences between those who lived in a crowded city ghetto and those in a rural, remote *shtetl*, those who chose to remain in Europe and those who sought a new and, they hoped, safer and more prosperous life in the United States, those whose political biases led them to improve conditions in their countries of origin and those who established a new country on the remains of the ancient Jewish homeland.

But the one thing that bound them together was the Yiddish language.

Bodily Functions

Quite a few expressions have to do with evacuation of bodily fluids (a nice way of saying "crapping, pissing, and barfing").

Brekhn
Vomit.

Me ken brekhn.
It can make you vomit.

Cristiyah
Enema.

I'd rather eat a box of prunes than have a *cristiyah*.

Dusn
Literally, this; euphemism for shit.

What a mess! Clean up the *dusn*.

Greps
Belch, burp, heart burn.

I love peppers but they give me *greps*.

Kaneh
An enema.

He was so embarrassed before his surgery when they had to give him a *kaneh*.

Pishekhts
Urine.

I wish my boyfriend would learn how to aim. The bathroom always smells like *pishekhts*.

Pishn
To urinate.

Ikh darf zikh oyspishn.
I have to take a leak.

Oy, ikh darf zikh oyspishn—geferlekh!
Boy, do I need to take a leak something fierce!

There are, of course, functions that nothing to do with elimination.

Bankes
Blood.

Toyten bankes.
Toyten *mean dead and the word* bankes *also referred to suction cups used medically to bring the blood to the surface.*

Es vet helfen vi a toyten bankes.
It will help like taking blood from a corpse.

Deige
Worry, concern.

Melokheh bez deigeh.
To have a trade is to be free of worry.

Eyn deige.
Literally, *one worry;* figuratively, *health.*
He goes to doctors all the time. He's obsessed with his ain deige.

Nit gedeiget.
Not to worry.
I panicked when my mother called me at midnight, but she said,
"Nit gedeiget. Everything's fine."

Kvitsh
Shriek, screech.

She gave a loud *kvitsh* when she saw that rat.

Shluf
Sleep.

Gai shlufn.
Go to sleep.

Shmeikhl
Literally, smile; figuratively, smooth talk.

He has such a beatific *shmeikhl* that it's easy to fall for his *shtik*.

His *shmeikhl* almost convinced me to go out with him.

Shokl
Rock back and forth rhythmically; used to describe movement during prayer.

Stand still and don't *shokl*. You're not in *shul*.

Shpilkes
Literally, nails; figuratively, to be impatient.

I can't take my husband to see a "chick flick." He gets *shpilkes*.

Sitzflaish
Literally, sitting flesh; figuratively, patience.

It is going to be a long wait. We'll need some *sitzflaish* or we'll get *shpilkes*.

Jewish Fashion

It should not be surprising that many of the words for items of clothing have a religious basis, as religion was central to Jewish life in Eastern Europe. It was just a fact of life, not a matter of philosophical or theological discussion, for all but the Talmudic scholars and their students. A married woman did not consider the feminist implications of keeping her hair covered in the presence of men other than her husband. The kind of clothing a man wore could identify him at a glance as belong to a particular Chasidic sect.

Gatkes
This word describes an article of clothing that is not religious, but is necessary in a cold climate: long underwear.

I was so glad I put on my *gatkes* before going out today, or I'd have frozen my *tuches* off.

Kapote

Long coat, kaftan (but not the kind that large size women wear when they want to be comfortable).

The *kapote* some ultra-Orthodox men wear is modeled on the clothing worn by medieval Polish nobility. And some of them look as though that's how old they are.

Kittel

A plain white robe, made of cotton or linen, worn on the High Holy Days. A groom who is traditional will often wear a *kittel* for the ceremony.

He's so cheap, he wore a *kittel* when he got married, even though he's not Orthodox. That way he got out of hiring a tux!

Pai'is

Side curls worn by Chasidic men in obedience to the law in the *Torah* not to cut the corners of one's beard.

When he goes out in public, he tucks his *pai'is* behind his ears. It seems hypocritical to me.

Shaitl

A wig worn by Orthodox women after they marry.

I don't understand how a *shaitl* can be a sign of modesty when some of them are sexier looking than the woman's real hair!

Tichel

A headscarf.

Instead of cutting her hair short and wearing a *shaitl*, she covers her head with a *tichel* when she's in public. She thinks she looks like a hippie, but she just looks odd.

Yarmulke

A skullcap, worn by Jews during worship or by Orthodox Jews all the time.

It's a *yarmulke*, not a beanie.

In Western culture, it is traditional for men to remove their hats indoors or in the presence of superiors, to show respect and/or humility. In Eastern cultures, a head covering is a symbol of reverence and/or subservience, often to God. When the two cultures collide, misunderstandings, discrimination, and persecution can result. In 1986, for example, the Supreme Court ruled in favor of the Air Force, which forbade a Jewish chaplain from wearing a yarmulke *while in uniform.*

Shmatte

A rag; used to refer to clothing. The word lent itself to a whole industry.

Put on a nice dress. You are not wearing that s*hmatte* on the first day of school.

Family Matters

And family does matter.

Ainikl

Grandchild.

She hopes her *ainikl* will give her son as much trouble as he gave her.

Bubbe and zaide

Grandmother and grandfather.

When your parents say, "No," ask your *bubbe*. If she says, "No," ask your *zaide*. He is a real pushover.

The word "bubbe" is also the source of the phrase *bubbe meises*, literally "grandmother stories," which refers to old wives' tales.

It's a *bubbe meise* that you'll catch a cold if you go outside without wearing a coat.

Bubele

A casual term of endearment, often used by people who are trying to establish an ersatz intimacy.

Listen, *bubele*, I wouldn't lie to you. You won't find a better deal anywhere.

Ganze mishpokha

The whole family.

Instead of enjoying his surprise birthday party, he got angry because the *ganze mishpokha* wasn't invited.

Mein tayerer kadishl

Literally, my dear little *Kaddish*.

After having given birth to several daughters, his wife finally gave him a *kadishl*.

Mein tayerer kadishl is about to become a father himself.

The Kaddish is known as the Mourner's Prayer, even though it is actually a paean of praise to God. It is recited by the deceased's closest relatives, mainly the spouse, the children, and siblings, although friends will often say it as well, especially during shiva, *the seven days of mourning following the funeral. Traditionally,* kaddish *was recited by males only, so* kaddishl *was an ironic way of referring to sons.*

Kindelakh

Little children.

I love having my cousins visit, but their *kindelakh* are out of control.

Mamaleh

Little mother, used as a term of endearment or exasperation.

Look at her taking care of her doll. Such a sweet *mamaleh*.

Hey, *mamaleh*, move your cart out of the middle of the aisle.

Oy, mamaleh, I got such a headache, you would not believe!

Tante

Aunt, can be used for a blood relative or for a close friend of one's parents.

I've never been able to figure out who's an aunt, who's a cousin, and who's my mother's friend. Eveyone one is called *tante*.

Tateh

Father.

My *tateh* was nothing like Ozzie Nelson!

Tateh-Mama

Literally, father-mother; refers to parents.

Barukh Hashem, my *tateh-mama* are still healthy.

She has a great relationship with her *tateh-mama*; they live on the other side of the country.

Yingele

Youngster.

You're too old to shovel the snow yourself. Hire the *yingele* next door to do it for you.

Yortzeit

Literally, time of year; refers to the anniversary of a death.

He forgot his father's *yortzeit* and his mother won't talk to him. To him, that's a *mekhei'ya*.

Yiddishe Mama

Literally, a Jewish mother, but refers more to a specific type of woman: warm, nurturing, and a bit smothering.

Gertrude Berg in the early '50s TV show *The Goldbergs* was the first *Yiddishe Mama* most of Middle America had ever invited into their living rooms.

One of the most beloved Yiddish songs of all time is "A Yiddish Mama," written by composer Jack Yellin and lyricist Lou Pollack. It produces the same sentimental reaction in Jewish listeners as "Danny Boy" does in Irish ones.

Miscellaneous

Bentsh
To make a blessing, usually after meals or over candles, but can be used as well in curses.

After spending the summer at a Jewish camp, my son began to *bentsh* after meals. But he didn't know the words, so it sounded like gibberish.

Got zol im bentshn mit dray mentshn: ainer zol im haltn, der tsvaiter zol im shpaltn un der driter zol im ba'haltn.
God should bless him with three people: one should grab him, the second should stab him, and the third should hide him.

Der zach
Literally, the thing; figuratively, whatchamacallit.

Hand me the … er … you know what I mean, *der zach* over there.

Emes
Truth.

A halber emes iz a gantzer ligen.
A half truth is a whole lie.

A ligen tor men nit zogen; dem emes iz men nit mekuyev zogen.
A lie shouldn't be told; the truth doesn't have to be told.

A ligner glaibt men nit, afileh az er zogt dem emes.
No one believes a liar even when he tells the truth.

Der emes hot a sakh ponimer.
The truth has many faces.

Di ergsteh rekhiles iz der emes.
The worst libel is the truth.

Ganze Megillah

The whole story, in detail. The word *megillah* is Hebrew for scroll, and is most often used to refer to the Book of Esther (*Megillas Ester*).

I made the mistake of asking him what he did on his vacation, and I got stuck listening to him for an hour as he gave me the *ganze Megillah*.

Get

Divorce decree, issued by rabbinic authorities to dissolve a marriage.

A week after the wedding, and he already wanted to give her a *get*.

Glatt azoy

Plainly, just so, for no reason.

Why do I want to take dance lessons? No particular reason, *glatt azoy*.

In mitn drinen

In the middle of.

The professor was telling us what would be on the final when *in mitn drinen* there was a fire drill.

Likht

Light; holiday or *Shabbos* candles.

Every Friday night, my mother would *bentch likht*. Then we'd go out to dinner.

Luftmensh

Someone who walks with his head in the air, a dreamer (but not an airhead).

My philosophy professor is a real *luftmensh*. He'll stop talking in the middle of a lecture because he's thought of something different, and then he'll walk out of the class-room muttering to himself. He doesn't even remember we're still in class.

Mensh

Literally, a man, but used to refer to a particular type of man, one who has a good heart and puts others first.

If he'd been a *mensh*, he'd have offered to use his snow blower on his neighbors' driveway. But he didn't.

As an adjective, the word is *menshlich*. *Menshlichkeit* describes the essence of what a *mensh* is.

I heard you took up a collection to buy Christmas gifts for your neighbor's kids when he got laid off. That was a *menshlich* thing to do.

It is *menshlichkeit* to do things because they are the right things to do, not because you want to get recognition for doing them.

Meshugana

Crazy, nuts.
Anything that drives you *meshugana* is *meshugas*, which has a connotation of nonsense.

I can't wait until the elections are over. All these campaign ads are driving me *meshugana*.

What do you mean you want to take a year off from college to be a roadie for a rock band? Stop talking such *meshugas*.

Meshuga zol er vern un arumloyfn iber di gasn.
He should go nuts and run around through the streets.

Ven dos volt nit geven mein meshugener, volt ikh oykh gelakht!
If he were not my madman, [if he were not related to me], I'd laugh at him, too.

Meshuge af toyt

Literally, crazy to death; figuratively, really nuts.

I can't wait for the winter break to be over. Those kids are making me *meshuge af toyt*.

Minyan

The quorum of ten adults required to have a full prayer service.

The members of the synagogue are getting older, and their *kindelakh* are moving to newer neighborhoods. They couldn't read the *Torah* today because they didn't have a *minyan*.

The minyan *used to consist only of men over the age of thirteen. Beginning in the late 1950s, women began to be counted as well. Now all but the most traditional synagogues include women in the* minyan.

Moyel

The person who makes the male *kindelakh* Jewish, the ritual circumciser who officiates at the *bris* (circumcision) of an eight-day-old infant boy or of an adult male convert to Judaism. The word is sometimes seen spelled as *mohel*.

I thought he was going to faint when he saw the *moyel* approach his baby with a scalpel.

Queen Victoria believed her family descended from King David, and decreed that her son Prince Albert was to be circumcised in accordance with Jewish tradition. Since then, until the latest generation, the British royal family has always used a moyel. *Prince Charles was circumcised by Rabbi Jacob Snowman, official Mohel of the London Jewish community. His children, however, were not snipped, possibly because Princess Diana was opposed to the practice, which is out of fashion in England.*

Shteebl

A small synagogue.

Every time someone would have a fight with the rabbi, he'd start his own *shteebl*.

Takhlis

Purpose, aim, heart of the matter.

I hate these meetings that go on and on with everybody having to give a long-winded speech. I wish they'd get down to *tachlis* already.

Takeh

An interjection with the sense of "Really?"

So, *takeh*, what happened on your blind date? I want the *emes*.

Vo den?

"What then?"

Vo den? Don't leave me in suspense. Finish the story.

Vos macht du?

Literally, What makes you? In other words, "How are you?"

I haven't seen you in ages. *Vos macht du*?

Yahupitz

Middle of nowhere, Hicksville.

I have no idea where they live, somewhere in *yahupitz*.

APPENDICES

I. What Is Yiddish Anyway?

First, let's look at what Yiddish is not. It is not Hebrew. It is not German written in Hebrew letters. It is not the *lingua franca* of the Jewish people. It is not a dead language.

In actuality, it is all of those things to some extent, but with exceptions, explanations, and a lot of "Yes, but's."

It is not Hebrew. Yes, but . . . it does have a lot of Hebrew words, although pronounced differently from the modern Hebrew of Israel. *Shabbos*, for example, is the Yiddish-inflected Eastern European (Ashkenazi) pronunciation for *Shabbat*, the Sabbath. *Yontif* (pronounced with a short-o and short-i), the word for holiday, is *Yom Tov* (both words with a long-o) in Hebrew. Many other words have a Hebrew etymology. *Tuches*, buttocks, for example, is from the Hebrew *takhat*, under.

There are two different pronunciations of Hebrew—Ashkenazi and Sephardi. *Ashkenaz* was the name given to Central Europe, dominated by Germany. The plural noun *Ashkenazim* became generalized to apply to all Jews of Central or Eastern European descent, as opposed to the Sephardim, those who could trace their origins to the Iberian Peninsula before they were expelled from there by the Inquisition in 1492. With some exceptions, Ashkenazim came from Christian countries, and Sephardim from Moslem.

Settling in Moslem countries that spoke Arabic or other Semitic languages, the Sephardim retained what is considered to be the original pronunciation of Hebrew. The Hebrew pronunciation used by Ashkenazim changed over the centuries of living in the midst of a general population that spoke Teutonic or Slavic languages. The emphasis shifted from the last to the first syllable, and the pronunciation of certain hard consonants became soft, with, for example, the final "t" becoming "s."

When Hebrew was revived as the official language of Israel, the Sephardi pronunciation was adopted, although more traditionally religious Israelis from Central and Eastern Europe have retained the Ashkenazi pronunciation for prayer and study. Today, the Sephardi pronunciation is standard in almost all but Orthodox synagogues in the United States.

In a parallel development to Yiddish, Jews who lived in countries surrounding the Mediterranean or in the Middle East incorporated similar vernaculars using Spanish or Farsi or Arabic, and writing the new hybrid languages in Hebrew letters. A Jew from Yemen would have understood as much Yiddish as did the Amish in The Frisco Kid. *(Actually, a Yemenite Jew would understand less Yiddish than the Amish; the Amish speak German, so they can comprehend Yiddish words that are cognates of German.)*

It is not German written in Hebrew letters. Yes, but . . . it is a Teutonic language, although a separate one from German. According to the website of the Institute for Jewish Research (*yivo.com*), one theory of the origin of Yiddish is that it developed during the migration of Jews to Central Europe from further west and south during the tenth century. The language contains elements of Hebrew, French, Italian, and German. After Jews moved even further east in the late Middle Ages, Slavic languages such as Polish, Russian, and Latvian were incorporated. And still later, immigrants to the United States added English elements to Yiddish.

It is not the lingua franca *of the Jewish people*. Yes, but . . . it *was* the *lingua franca* of the Jews of Eastern Europe. It allowed Jews from different European countries, who may have spoken Russian but not Polish, or Latvian but not French, to converse with each other.

It is not a dead language. Yes, but . . . the number of Yiddish speakers, those who have spoken it from birth, is small. At its peak, before the Holocaust, it was the most widely spoken Jewish language, with an estimated ten to eleven million users; the number now is under two million, and few of them consider Yiddish their primary language.

On the night of August 12–13, 1952, five of the most prominent Yiddish poets living in the Soviet Union were secretly executed in the basement of the Lubyanka Prison in Moscow. Stalin had ordered the executions, claiming the poets, all of whom were associated with the Jewish Anti-Fascist Committee, established by Stalin in 1942 to enlist the aid of the Allied nations' Jewish communities in the Soviet struggle again Hitler, were spies and traitors.

In some Orthodox and Chasidic communities in the United States and elsewhere, including Israel, Yiddish is still used for everyday speech, with English (or Hebrew) as a second language. In the United States, the dialectical combination of Yiddish and English spoken by the ultra Orthodox is sometimes referred to rather disparagingly as "Yeshivish." The Yiddish words are written in the Latin alphabet and the English ones are spoken with a Yiddish syntax and inflection. The Orthodox in Israel, however, generally use both standard Yiddish and colloquial Hebrew, although the pronunciation is the Ashkenazic not the Sephardic of modern Hebrew; e.g., they say *Shabbos*, not *Shabbat*.

From the earliest days of Zionism, debate raged over whether Hebrew or Yiddish should be the language of the Jewish Homeland. (The arguments in favor of Yiddish seemed to have ignored the large population of Sephardim to whom Yiddish was even more foreign than modern Hebrew.)

The ultra Orthodox in Israel reject the use of Hebrew for anything except study and prayer, and refuse to speak anything but Yiddish or other secular languages for mundane, everyday communication. The plaque outside the Jerusalem home of Eliezer ben Yehuda (1858–1922), the "Father of Modern Hebrew," the man credited with almost single handedly reviving Hebrew as a spoken language, is regularly vandalized or removed, presumably by those who believe the use of Hebrew for worldly commerce is a desecration of the *loshn kodesh*, holy language.

In the United States and other Western countries, the successful assimilation of the Eastern European Jewish immigrants meant that the following generations did not know Yiddish. The language was virtually eradicated in Europe by the murder of the majority of its speakers in the Holocaust. Stalin and other leaders of the USSR destroyed much of its remnants, particularly literary.

An example of the decline—or evolution, perhaps—of the everyday use of Yiddish can be seen by looking at the history of Jewish newspapers, particularly the *Forverts*. A daily

Yiddish-language socialist-leaning newspaper, the *Forverts* was the main source of news, gossip, advice, literature, culture, and entertainment for new immigrants and their children.

From 1885 to 1914, over 150 Yiddish publications—dailies, weeklies, monthlies, quarterlies—were established in New York City alone. Twenty of these New York publications were daily newspapers, with as many as six in existence competing with each other at a time. During the year 1915–16, there were five dailies in New York City with a circulation of 500,000 readers. Abraham Cahan, the founder and editor of the *Forverts* until his death in 1950, wrote, "The five million Jews living under the czar had not a single Yiddish daily paper even when the government allowed such publication, while [we] in America publish six dailies, [plus] countless Yiddish weeklies and monthlies. . . . New York [is] the largest Yiddish book market in the world."

When the *Forverts* published its first issue on April 22, 1897, there were thirteen Yiddish newspapers in the United States. Within twenty years, it had become the largest of them, with a circulation of 275,000. (By comparison, *La Prensa*, the New York-based daily Spanish newspaper, the largest foreign language newspaper in the United States, has a circulation of 250,000.) In addition, it had twelve metropolitan editions in cities from Boston to Los Angeles, with a readership of another quarter of a million. Circulation began to decline after the passage of restrictive immigration quotas in 1923, and continued to fall. Almost a century after its founding, it became a weekly in 1983 and added a supplement in English. Seven years after that adaptation, it evolved into an English-language weekly, *The Forward*, and published a separate Yiddish supplement. *The Forward* still publishes *tseitung romans* (literally, "newspaper novels," the phrase refers to novels serialized in newspapers, such as Charles Dickens' works when they were first published), but they are now in the English of Anne Roiphe, not in the Yiddish of Isaac Bashevis Singer.

One interesting feature the Forverts *ran was called* A Gallarya fon Fahrshvondne Manner, *translated as* *"A Gallery of Disappeared Husbands." Often, the men would emigrate first, in order to earn money and become established before sending tickets for their wives and children to follow. Sometimes, they came to enjoy the freedoms of being a bachelor in this new world too much, and did not want to go back to the restrictions of married life. Their wives would list their names in the* Forverts, *along with their pictures, to embarrass them into fulfilling their familial responsibilities. The movie* Hester Street *is an excellent portrayal of the cultural clash between the Americanized husband and the Old World wife who joins him later in New York.*

The English weekly's circulation is around 26,000, and the Yiddish edition is around 3,000. The mission of the *Forverts* was to Americanize the new Jewish immigrants. The decline in circulation in a sense was a testament to its success.

The earlier Yiddish newspapers often ran stories they either made up themselves (a la Hearst) or cribbed from the general circulation press. The *Philadelphia Yiddish Weekly* once misinterpreted the headline in the shipping page of an English language paper that read "The Empress of China Arrived Yesterday on Her Maiden Voyage." The editor, Hayim Malitz, thought the headline meant that China's unmarried queen had come to Philadelphia to find a husband, and ran a story to that effect.

The most famous of the features in the *Forverts* was *A Bintel Brief*, literally, "a bundle of letters," an advice column that set the model for all the advice columnists to follow. Abraham Cahan answered questions that reflected the new immigrants' bewilderment at American mores and customs. The concerns addressed covered all aspects of life, from unemployment to marital problems to conflicts with children who rejected the Old World customs of their parents. Today, the *Bintel Brief* continues—as "The Bintel Blog."

Pronouncements of the death of Yiddish, however, have been premature. Yes, it is an academic discipline that is studied, researched, and taught at the college level. Yes, much of its rich literature is known only in translation, or in "sanitized" Broadway versions. Yet, despite its reputation as a scholarly pursuit or quaint anachronism, it continues to be spoken and, more importantly, to evolve. And to Jews whose ancestors came from Eastern Europe, even for those who speak no Yiddish at all, it still remains the *mameloshn*, mother tongue.

II. Yiddish Culture

Literature

Until the mid-nineteenth century, most Yiddish literature was in the form of folk tales, parables, ethical tales, and legends. The Chasidim in particular used parables to disseminate the teachings of their *rebbes*, who were a combination of rabbi, spiritual leader, advisor, and teacher. Some proponents of the *Haskalah* (Enlightenment) wrote their own novels and plays to counteract these Chasidic legends.

Because Hebrew was used only for prayer and religious study in Eastern Europe, women, who were not required to pray three times a day or engage in religious study, generally knew only enough Hebrew to be able to say the blessings connected with the home and with ritual purity. They had their own holy book, however, called Tsena U'rena *("Come Out and Look"), which contained Yiddish translations of the weekly Torah and Haftarah portions, plus Yiddish commentaries, stories, and parables based on them.*

Zikhroynes Glikl Hamel (*The Memoirs of Gluckl of Hamlin*) is generally considered to be the first full-length Yiddish book. Born in 1646 in Hamburg, Gluckl married a businessman, and, while helping him run his business, raised twelve children. After he left her a widow at age forty-three, she took complete control of his business, and traveled extensively through Central Europe. The diaries, which were left to her children after her death in 1724 in Metz, provide a detailed look at Jewish life in Central Europe during the late eighteenth century. They were not published until 1892.

The name Sholem Aleichem is taken from the phrase used when two Jews greet each other. It means "peace upon you," and the proper response is aleikhem sholem, "upon you peace." In the original stories, Shprintze, one of Tevye's seven daughters (there are five in Fiddler on the Roof*) falls in love with a rich young man, whose uncle thinks she is after his money. He will not allow the marriage, the young man leaves, and Shprintze throws herself into the river and drowns. Tevye's son-in-law Motl becomes ill and suddenly dies. Tevye's wife Golde dies of natural causes. Chava's non-Jewish husband, rather than casting his fate with the Jews, beats Chava, who leaves him and is accepted back into the family. The writing gene passed on through the generations, as Bel Kaufman, author of "Up the Down Staircase," was Sholem Aleichem's granddaughter.*

Dos Klaine Mentshele (*The Little Person*), published in 1864, is generally considered the first modern Yiddish book. It was written by Sholem Yankev Abramovitsh, who became known as Mendele Moykher Sforim ("Mendel the Book Peddler"), the fictional narrator of many of his stories. He, along with Sholem Rabinovitsh (better known by his penname, Sholem Aleichem) and I. L. Peretz, formed the triumvirate that epitomized Yiddish literature. They are collectively known as *di klasiker* (the classics).

Of the three *klasiker*, Sholem Aleichem is the best known to English speakers because of the popularity of the adaptation of his series of short stories, "Tevye and His Daughters." The original story is much darker and more tragic than the Broadway or Hollywood musical versions called *Fiddler on the Roof*.

The most prolific years of Yiddish literature were 1900–1940, but it continues to this day. Isaac Bashevis Singer is one of the best known of the more modern Yiddish writers, in part because of the movie adaptation of his short story "Yentl der Yeshiva Bokher" (Yentl, the Yeshiva Boy.)

Similar to the "sanitizing" that took place when Sholem Aleichem's stories about Tevye the Dairyman were transformed into *Fiddler on the Roof*, Singer's original short is more explicitly sexual than Barbra Streisand's movie version. In both a 1975 English-language stage adaptation written by Singer and Leah Napolin and in the original on which it is based,Yentl tells her study partner, who discovers her real sex, that she is "neither one sex nor the other" and has "the soul of a man in the body of a woman." Many in the gay, lesbian, and transgender community take this statement to mean that Yentl was not a proto-feminist (the implication of the movie), but a transgendered person, in part because at the end of the story, Yentl decides to continue to live her life as her male alter ego.

In 1978, Isaac Bashevis Singer won the Nobel Prize for Literature, the only Yiddish writer to have done so, not only assuring his legacy but that of Yiddish literature in general.

Theater

Not surprisingly, Yiddish theater flourished during the same period as Yiddish literature. All the various genres of plays were represented, from broad farce to melodrama, from musical revues to experimental theater, from Yiddish translations of Shakespeare (*King Lear* and *Hamlet* were particularly popular) to political satire.

Yiddish theaters existed in every large (and not-so-large) community where there were Jews. Following the 1881 assassination of Tsar Alexander II, whose reign had been marked by the relaxation of many harsh laws against the Jews, there was a backlash against his pro-Semitic rulings, and by 1883, Yiddish theaters were banned in Imperial Russia. The ban was not lifted until 1904, by which time Yiddish theater had moved to Western Europe and to the United States, where it grew and prospered. Just before World War I, there were twenty-two Yiddish theaters and two Yiddish vaudeville houses in New York City, while over two hundred Yiddish theaters were founded throughout the United States between 1890 and 1940.

The Holocaust brought an end to Yiddish theater in Europe, and assimilation and the ascendency of Hebrew curtailed its popularity elsewhere. Today, the State Jewish Theater of Bucharest, Romania, considered the birthplace of Yiddish theater (Abraham Goldfaden established the first professional Yiddish acting troupe there in 1876), still produces some Yiddish plays, but with simultaneous Romanian translation. In Israel, the Yiddishpiel Theatre company, which was founded in 1987, presents new Yiddish plays. In North America, the Dora Wasserman Yiddish Theatre of Montreal, established in 1958, and the Folksbiene (People's Stage) Yiddish Theatre of New York, founded in 1915, are still producing Yiddish plays.

Film

Yiddish films are not as numerous as theatrical plays were. In the years between the two World Wars, approximately one hundred

Yiddish films were produced. Four of them, made in Poland by Joseph Green, have become classics, especially the two which starred Molly Picon, *Yidl Mitn Fidl* (*The Little Jew with a Fiddle*, 1936), in which she plays a young woman who disguises herself as a man so she can join a band of traveling musicians; and *Mamele* (*The Little Mother*, 1938) in which she is responsible for raising her brothers and sisters after the death of her mother. Both are musical comedies. The other two Green films are *Der Purimspiler* (*The Jester*, 1937), a romantic comedy, and *A Brivele der Mamen* (*A Letter to Mama*, 1938), a sentimental melodrama.

Many of the Yiddish films were adaptations of Yiddish literary works, such as "The Dybbuk," but many others were melodramas, comedies, or musicals. *Shund* (trash) was as popular a genre for movies as it was for plays.

Yiddish film did not survive either the Holocaust or the decline of Yiddish as a spoken language. In a 1991 documentary, Green, then ninety-one years old, said, "Six million of my best customers perished."

Actors
Many veterans of the Yiddish theater made successful transitions to the English-language stage (and film and TV). One of the giants of Yiddish theater Jacob Adler, known as the "Great Eagle" (*adler* is German for eagle), began his career in Russia, gained fame in London, and was idolized in the United States. In 1903, his fame reached international superstar status after he received rave reviews as Shylock in the Broadway production of *The Merchant of Venice.*

Another great of the Yiddish theater, Boris Tomashevsky, did not make the transition to the English-language stage. Unlike

Adler, who preferred serious dramas, Tomashevsky starred in what was disparagingly referred to as *shund* (trash) plays—melodramas, farces, and other light works. Tomashevsky's grandson is the renowned conductor Michael Tilson-Thomas.

Jacob Adler's daughter Stella was the only American actor to have been trained by Stanislavski in what became known as Method Acting. She founded an acting school that still bears her name (and reputation). His brother, Luther Adler, also gained fame in English-language plays and films after being in the Yiddish theater.

Many Yiddish actors did make the crossover from Yiddish theater to English-language productions. They include:

- Reizl Bozyk, mainly a Yiddish actor, was the Bubbe in *Hester Street.*
- Joseph Buloff had roles in many television shows as well as movies. One of his last roles, only two years before his death in 1985 at age eighty-six, was in the movie *Reds.*
- Fyvush Finkel had several roles in television and films before becoming beloved as a regular on the television series *Picket Fences.*
- Leo Fuchs was a character actor who got his start in 1950.
- Estelle Getty, "Sophia" on *The Golden Girls,* got her start in the Yiddish theater and in the Borscht Belt.
- Sam Jaffe, despite his numerous roles, will always be known as Dr. Zorba in *Ben Casey.*

- Sidney Lumet, best known as a director, made his stage debut at age four in the Yiddish Art Theater in New York.
- Walter Matthau, who, despite looking like a sad bloodhound, always managed to woo and win the likes of Sophia Loren and Goldie Hawn, got his start in the Yiddish theater at age eleven.
- Paul Muni, one of only six actors to receive an Oscar nomination as Best Actor in a Lead Role for his first movie (in *The Valiant*, 1929), was nominated five more times and won for *The Story of Louis Pasteur*, in 1935.
- Leonard Nimoy, forever known as Mr. Spock from the *Star Trek* franchise, worked in a Yiddish theater group when he first moved to Los Angeles.
- David Opatoshu, who got his start in the Yiddish theater, won an Emmy in 1990 for Outstanding Guest Actor in a Drama Series for his role in *Gabriel's Fire.*
- Molly Picon, who at the age of eighty-six acted in "Cannonball Run II," was a star not only of the Yiddish theater but of Yiddish films.
- Menasha Skulnik, a luminary of the Yiddish theater, won a Tony for Best Actor in a Musical for his performance in the Broadway play *The Zulu and the Zayda*, in 1964.
- Harold J. Stone, a character actor who had supporting roles in numerous films and television shows, started on the stage as a child with his father, a Yiddish actor.

Music

Much Jewish music was either liturgical (many of the great Jewish opera singers were trained as cantors) or instrumental. The only musical genres that can be called Yiddish are folksongs, lullabies, show tunes, and popular songs with Yiddish lyrics. *Klezmer*, a type of music played at weddings and other celebrations, is often called "Yiddish," but is more properly described as Eastern European Jewish because it is mainly instrumental.

The word *klezmer*, from the Hebrew *klai zemer*, (vessels of song, musical instruments), refers to Eastern European Jewish itinerant musicians and to their musical instruments. *Klezmorim* (the plural form of the word) were looked down upon by the religious because of their secular way of life. They often traveled with the Romany, and there are influences of each musical form in the other's music.

Klezmer *music has been compared to Dixieland and has been called "Jewish jazz." With its reliance on brass instruments like the clarinet, it also influenced modern composers like Aaron Copeland, Leonard Bernstein, and George Gershwin (particularly the opening bars of "Rhapsody in Blue"), as well as Big Band clarinetist Benny Goodman.*

The mid-to-late twentieth century saw a "klez revival." Unlike traditional *klezmer* music, the contemporary groups include singing, and many of the songs have English lyrics. In 2006, the Klezmatics, one of the most popular bands of the klez revival, recorded "Woodie Guthrie's Happy Joyous Hannukah," which set Guthrie's words to *klezmer* music. That same year, they won the Grammy for Contemporary World Music for their album *Wonder Wheel,* in which they set lyrics written by Guthrie when he lived in the Coney Island section of Brooklyn to various musical genres, including *klezmer*.

III. A Note on Transliterations

Yiddish is a Germanic language written in Hebrew characters. As with any transliteration, there are always inaccuracies in trying to describe how a word sounds. But there are also problems because of regional pronunciations. In English, for example, is the word "aunt" to be transliterated as "ant" or "ahnt"? Is the opening diphthong in "either" pronounced as long-e or long-i?

In Yiddish, is *kugel*, a pudding made from noodles, potato, or matzo, pronounced *kiggel* (as in Galicia, the part of the Austro-Hungarian Empire that changed its nationality depending on who had won the previous war) or *koogel* (as in Lithuania)? More than one Galitzianer-Litvak intermarried family has been rent asunder by this debate. In the case of *kugel*, there is general agreement that the dish is transliterated into English as *kugel*, even though it is pronounced differently depending on family tradition and country of origin. Not so with other Yiddish words, however. In the case of unleavened bread, *matzo* is the spelling most commonly seen on supermarket boxes, but *matzah* and *matzoh* are occasionally seen, too. And there are as many spellings in English of the winter Holiday of Lights as there are days of the holiday: *Hanukkah, Hannukkah, Hanuka, Hannukka, Chanukah, Channukah, Chanuka, Channukka*.

Only *Hanukkah* and *Chanukah* are considered normative transliterations, but neither one accurately describes the pronunciation of the first letter. The word in Hebrew is neither an aspirated *h* as in "hello," nor is it *ch* as in "China." The guttural sound is most like the German *ach*, which can be rendered in English as *kh*. However, seldom (if ever) will the transliteration *Khanukah* appear (with or without doubled consonants or final *h*) in English. (Linguistically, the letter should be written with a dot under an *h* or a dot over a *k*.)

For words in this book, I have generally maintained the transliteration spellings that are considered scholarly, except when those spellings are difficult for English-speaking readers to decipher. For example, I have retained *ch* for familiar words such as *tuches* (rear end), even though it has a guttural sound. Another exception is *challah*, the egg bread used on the Sabbath. Not only is it familiar to English speakers, but to spell it phonetically as *khallah* would make it look too much like the word for "bride," *kallah*. For other, less familiar words, I did use *ch* for the soft sound, and *kh* for the guttural. (For example, the slow-cooking stew, a traditional Sabbath afternoon dish, called *cholent*, is pronounced with the soft *ch* sound.)

In addition, I changed the academic transliterations of Yiddish words that have found their way into English usage. *Shmuck* (slang for penis, used in English as a derisive term similar to "asshole"), for example, is properly transliterated as *shmok*, and the above-mentioned *tuches* as *tokhes*. But those words look strange to eyes used to American pronunciations of Yiddish. In the same way, I have used "tz" instead of the preferred "ts" since many of the words, such as *mitzvah, matzo, blintz,* are familiar to English-speakers. Also, the "ts" transliteration would make some words look like a common English one; e.g., *putz* should be properly transliterated as "pots."

It is standard to use "k" instead of "ck," and I have done so except when the "ck" is more familiar. For consistency, I have used "sh" throughout the book, even when word processing software accept some Yiddish words when they are spelled "sch," but not "sh." The only exceptions are names based on Yiddish words and words like *borscht* (Russian) and *kitsch* (German).

For vowel sounds, I have transliterated long-a as "ai," (*maidl*— young woman); long-i as "ei" (*bubbe meise*—a fairy tale); long-e as "ee" (*meeskeit*—someone homely), except when a different spelling is familiar to English-speakers.

In other words, do not look for a consistent transliteration scheme!

IV. Yiddish Grammar

Although this is not a how-to-speak-Yiddish book, it is important to understand some basic grammatical rules. These are general ones, as it is outside the scope of this book to get into grammatical details, irregular nouns and verbs, and all the other idiosyncrasies of a spoken language.

Unlike English, but like most other languages, the nouns are male, female, and neuter, and the verbs, adjectives, and articles agree with the gender. There are several different plural endings for nouns: *–n*, *–en*, *–er*, *–s*, *–es*.

For adjectives, the masculine ending is *–er*, while the feminine, the neuter, and the plural are all *–e*.

The definite articles are *der* (masculine), *di* (feminine), and *dos* (neuter) for singular nouns. All plural nouns take the feminine, *di*. The indefinite article is *a*, the same as in English.

Yiddish is a Teutonic language, but because of the influence of Slavic languages differs from it in a few ways. Unlike German, for example, the verb in Yiddish generally follows the subject, in the same manner as in English, rather than being at the end of the sentence as in German. There are, of course, exceptions, but most of those have to do with emphasis. (The same is true in conversational English: A polite invitation—"Do you want to go to dinner with me?"—can become one of incredulity—"*Me*, you want to go to dinner with?")

Like German and English, but unlike some Romance languages such as Italian, the adjective precedes the noun in Yiddish. (Interestingly, in Hebrew, the other language of the Jews, but with a Semitic origin, and one which has nothing to do with Yiddish except the etymology of some words in both languages and the alphabet used, the adjective follows the noun.)

In Yiddish, infinitive verbs take the ending *–n* or *–en*. The past participle is formed by adding *ge–* at the beginning and *–n*, *–en*, or *–t* at the end. The past tense is formed by adding *hoben* (to have) or *zein* (to be) before the past participle. In the present tense, verbs are conjugated for person and number by the addition of suffixes: the base word (without the infinitive *–n* suffix) in the first person; *–st* in the second person singular; *–t* in the neuter singular and the second person plural; *–n* in the first and third person plurals.

One standard feature of Yiddish, which it shares with Greek, Hebrew, and most Romance and Slavic languages, but interestingly not with most Teutonic languages, is the use of double negatives. The expression *nit kain* (not none) is used frequently.

Bibliography

Allen, Woody. *The Insanity Defense: The Complete Prose*. (New York, NY: Random House, 2007).

___. *Mere Anarchy*. (New York, NY: Random House, 2007).

Ayto, John, & Ian Crofton. *Brewer's Dictionary of Modern Phrase and Fable*. (New York, NY: Sterling Publishing Co., 2006).

Blech, Rabbi Benjamin. *Complete Idiot's Guide to Learning Yiddish*. (New York, NY: Alpha, 2002).

Emmes, Yetta. *Drek!: The Real Yiddish Your Bubbe Never Taught You*. (New York, NY: Plume, 1998).

Epstein, Lita. *If You Can't Say Anything Nice, Say It in Yiddish: The Book of Yiddish Insults and Curses*. (New York, NY: Citadel Press, 2006).

Franzos, Karl Emil. Michael Mitchell, translator. *Leib Weihnachtskuchen and His Child*. (Ariadne Press, 2005; originally published 1896).

Kogos, Fred. *From Shmear to Eternity: The Only Book of Yiddish You'll Ever Need*. (New York, NY: Citadel Press, 2006).

___. *The Dictionary of Yiddish Slang and Idioms*. (New York, NY: Citadel, 2002).

___. *The Dictionary of Popular Yiddish Words, Phrases and Proverbs*. (New York, NY: Citadel, 1997).

Loeffler, James. "*Di Rusishe Progresiv Muzikal Yunyon No. 1 Fun Amerike*: The First Klezmer Union In America - Klezmer: History And Culture," *Judaism* (Winter, 1998).

Peer, Janet. *Yiddish for Dogs*. (New York, NY: Hyperion, 2007).

Rosten, Leo. *Hooray for Yiddish!* (New York, NY: Simon & Schuster, 1982).

___. *The Joys of Yiddish*. (New York, NY: McGraw Hill, 1968).

___. *The New Joys of Yiddish*. Revised by Lawrence Bush. (New York, NY: Three Rivers Press, 2001)

Samuel, Maurice. *In Praise of Yiddish*. (New York, NY: Cowles Book Company, 1971).

Sinclair, Julian. *Let's Schmooze: Jewish Words Today*. (London: Continuum, 2007).

Singer, Joel. *May You . . . ! How to Curse in Yiddish*. (New York, NY: Ballantine, 1977).

Stevens, Payson R., Charles M. Levine, & Sol Steinmetz. *Meshuggenary: Celebrating the World of Yiddish*. (New York, NY: Simon & Schuster, 2002).

Vincent, Isabel. *Bodies and Souls: The Tragic Plight of Three Jewish Women Forced into Prostitution in the Americas*. (New York, NY: William Morrow, 2005).

Weiner, Ellis and Barbara Davilman. *Yiddish with George and Laura*. (New York, NY: Little, Brown, 2006).

Weinreich, Uriel. *Modern English-Yiddish, Yiddish-English Dictionary*. (New York, NY: Schocken Books, 1977).

Wex, Michael. *Born to Kvetch: Yiddish Language and Culture in All of Its Moods*. (New York, NY: Harper Perennial, 2006).

___. *Just Say* Nu*: Yiddish for Every Occasion (When English Just Won't Do)*. (New York, NY: St. Martin's Press, 2007).

www.about.com

www.answers.yahoo.com

www.ask.com

www.ariga.com/yiddish.shtml

www.bnaimitzvahguide.com/common.yiddish.terms.php

www.cjh.org

www.dictionary.reference.com

www.etymonline.com

www.forward.com

www.hebrew4christians.com/Glossary/Yiddish_Words /yiddish_words.html

www.imbd.com

www.jewish-languages.org

www.jewishvirtuallibrary.org

www.jewishworldreview.com

www.juf.org

www.koshernosh.com/dictiona.htm

www.lexicool.com/ectaco-online-dictionary.asp

www.lingvozone.com/Yiddish

www.myjewishlearning.com

www.mysite.verizon.net/jialpert/Yiddish/Glossary.htm

www.pass.to/glossary

www.tau.ac.il/~itamarez/works/papers/papers/lngconfl.htm

www.the-yiddish-world-of-michael-wex.com

www.uta.fi/FAST/US1/yidgloss.html

www.wordcraft.infopop.cc

www.worldwidewords.org/weirdwords/

www.yiddishdictionaryonline.com

www.yiddishisms.com

www.yivo.com

And fifty years of reading *Mad Magazine*

About the Author

Ilene Schneider is one of the first six women rabbis in the United States. She currently serves as the Coordinator of Jewish Hospice for Samaritan Hospice in Marlton, NJ, near Philadelphia. She is also the author of a mystery, *Chanukah Guilt*, which is the first of a series featuring Rabbi Aviva Cohen.